LINCOLN

How Abraham Lincoln Ended Slavery in America

A Companion Book
for Young Readers to the
Steven Spielberg Film
LINCOLN

LINCOLN

*How Abraham Lincoln
Ended Slavery in America*

HAROLD HOLZER

**newmarket press
for it books**
AN IMPRINT OF HARPERCOLLINS PUBLISHERS

To Charles

A teaching guide aligned with the Common Core State Standards will be available for download at www.HarperAcademic.com.

HarperCollins books may be purchased for educational, business, or sales promotional use. For information please e-mail the Special Markets Department at SPsales@harpercollins.com.

First Newmarket Press for It Books paperback edition published 2013.

Designed by Lorie Pagnozzi

Library of Congress Cataloging-in-Publication Data is available upon request.

ISBN 978-0-06-226511-1

13 14 15 16 17 OV/RRD 10 9 8 7 6 5 4 3 2 1

HURRAH FOR THE CHOICE OF THE NATION!

OUR CHIEFTAIN SO BRAVE AND SO TRUE;

WE'LL GO FOR THE GREAT REFORMATION—

FOR LINCOLN AND LIBERTY TOO!

—Words to a Lincoln campaign song, 1860

* CONTENTS *

★ INTRODUCTION ★

Some five or six years ago, I received one of the most exciting invitations that ever crossed my desk. The great director Steven Spielberg was asking: would I please join a group of Lincoln scholars—led by my friend historian Doris Kearns Goodwin—to spend an entire day talking about Abraham Lincoln. Would I? You bet!

Not long before, Mr. Spielberg had announced that he had acquired rights to Goodwin's book *Team of Rivals* and intended to turn it into a major film. The invitation to join an all-day meeting on Lincoln told me something very important: that the director was going to take this subject very seriously. He had obviously learned a good deal from Doris's bestseller. And now as he began thinking of what aspect to make the focus of his movie, he wanted to learn still more. With her typical generosity, Doris, too, was eager to get her friends and colleagues together.

And this was a generous offer indeed. The scholars would be flown in from all over the country, no matter where they lived, to meet at a luxurious hotel and share breakfast and lunch with Mr. Spielberg and his advisers. My only disappointment was that the meeting wouldn't take place in Hollywood. Instead, it was to be held in Manhattan, only a few blocks south of where I work at the Metropolitan Museum of Art. I wouldn't be flown to Tinseltown after all. I would take a taxi downtown to a building overlooking Central Park (so does *my* office!).

But the meeting proved amazing anyway. Mr. Spielberg was joined by both his producer and by the brilliant playwright Tony Kushner, who we learned had just signed on to write the screenplay for the new movie. I'll never forget looking on with fascination as Tony unpacked a small leather case, and took from it a full inkwell and some fountain pens, which he lined up in front of him. For the rest of the meeting, he took all his notes the old-fashioned way, with blue ink staining his fingers as he wrote. I expect he wrote the entire movie in this manner.

Over terrific food and wonderful conversation, the six or so of us talked that day about almost everything we knew of Abraham Lincoln: his boyhood, his education, his learning curve on the subject of slavery, his marriage, his children, his life in law and politics, his ability as an orator, and his genius at military strategy. Mr. Spielberg didn't know exactly what part of the Lincoln story he would focus on, so he wanted to hear as much as we would tell him. He sat at the center of a long table, a baseball cap pulled over his head, and asked question after probing question for hours. I like to think we rose to the occasion that day, because he told us the meeting was a real success and he finished it feeling more inspired about his project than ever. I think we only asked *him* one question all day: how would he film the Gettysburg Address? Would he do a close-up of Lincoln or show the big crowd that was listening to the president?

Here is where we learned the difference between history writing and moviemaking. Without a pause, Mr. Spielberg closed his eyes and began describing an alternative way of presenting the Gettysburg Address: maybe showing a group of children running around the outskirts of the vast audience while Lincoln tries to get the big crowd to hear him, maybe showing the autumn leaves falling from the trees in the wind, maybe not even focusing on Lincoln himself until the end—or maybe not at all.

We were amazed. No one in the room had ever thought of such an approach. Of course, we're not film directors. In the end, Mr. Spielberg chose an entirely different—but equally original—way to get Lincoln's most famous words into the movie. I like to think that we were at least present at the creation.

But there was more to come. In the years that followed, as the Lincoln community continued to buzz about the Spielberg movie, I continued to enjoy a tangential connection to the project, although I never met Mr. Spielberg again and saw Tony Kushner only at events and openings around New York. Happily, my own ongoing adventure with Spielberg's *Lincoln* included two more chapters. More than a year or two ago, Tony Kushner asked me to read a draft of his beautiful script and alert him to any possible factual errors. What a privilege it was to take the big red notebook home and read every word—twice. Errors? Very few and very minor, easy to fix. More importantly, I've never read a stage play or screenplay that more brilliantly captured the real Lincoln—his greatest accomplishments, his elusive personality, and the tension and drama of his final days in the White House.

Finally came one more irresistible invitation: the opportunity to write this book especially for young readers as a companion to the final film. It has been an unforgettable honor to have played even a tiny part in this effort to make history come alive. I can only hope this small book does justice to the geniuses who have brought the movie *Lincoln*—and for that matter Abraham Lincoln himself—to life.

—HAROLD HOLZER, AUGUST 2012

★ LINCOLN ★

How Abraham Lincoln Ended Slavery in America

✳ PROLOGUE ✳

A "KING'S CURE"
January 31, 1865

For weeks, President Abraham Lincoln had waited anxiously for Congress to act—waited, counted votes, held last-minute meetings, made promises, offered deals, and, when necessary, twisted arms. But now, as Lincoln sat in his corner office on the second floor of the White House, he could do nothing more than wait a bit longer for the news to come at last from Capitol Hill, a mile and a half away. Members of the Senate and House of Representatives were finally making their decision. Would the House vote to approve or reject a Thirteenth Amendment to the U.S. Constitution that would abolish slavery throughout the United States? The Constitution was the country's original and most important set of rules and laws. Many Americans believe the Constitution should never be altered, and no addition to it had been approved for more than six decades. Lincoln believed that after four years of civil war fought over the issue of human slavery, it was time to remove slavery from America forever.

Just a few months earlier, Lincoln had won a hard-fought campaign for reelection as president. In just a few weeks, he was scheduled to take the oath of office at his second inauguration. In the nerve-wracking days leading up to the historic vote, Lincoln had tried to conduct business as usual at the White House.

He welcomed a group of Philadelphia women who had raised great sums of money to care for wounded soldiers. He accepted the gift of a vase made of leaves gathered from the Gettysburg battlefield. He celebrated the Union capture of Wilmington, North Carolina. He began making plans to meet with Confederate leaders on the subject of peace. Lincoln even rode up to the Capitol himself—not to lobby for passage of the Thirteenth Amendment, but to attend a special concert in honor of the volunteers who helped nurse and feed the troops. There, the president was so touched when a singer named Philip Phillips offered an inspiring tune called "Your Mission," he asked to hear it sung one more time. Lincoln always loved a sentimental song. But even music did not make him less nervous about the country's future, or less determined to fulfill his own mission: to end slavery.

The president was exhausted. Lincoln seldom got to bed before midnight those days. He hardly got to see his family, ate too little, and worked himself nearly to death. He had too much on his schedule, and far too much on his mind. It was obvious to many that over the past year he had lost too much weight. His face looked gaunt. Although not yet fifty-six, Lincoln looked far older than his years.

And then came the glorious news. Months earlier, despite pressure from Lincoln, the House of Representatives had failed by a mere handful of votes to approve the Thirteenth Amendment to the Constitution. A two-thirds majority in both houses of Congress was required for the measure to go to the states for ratification. On the first try, the U.S. Senate had passed the amendment, but the forces of freedom had fallen short when it

The last photo of Lincoln—March 6, 1865—was taken on the White House balcony just days after Congress passed the Thirteenth Amendment. (Photo by Henry F. Warren, courtesy Library of Congress)

came to the House. This time, however, enough representatives changed their minds to change history. Lincoln had actually helped change some of those minds himself, an unusual exercise of power and persuasion for presidents of that time. But still he had not been sure he had done enough. Finally, on January 31, Congress voted to send the Thirteenth Amendment to the legislatures of all the states of the union. Now, if three-fourths of the states approved it, the amendment would become an official part of the U.S. Constitution—which had accepted the existence of human slavery since it was first created in 1787 and had added no new amendments of any kind since 1804.

The next day, February 1, 1865, a clerk brought to Lincoln's desk the official congressional resolution on passage of the Thirteenth Amendment. Lincoln read the document carefully. He was no doubt overjoyed by the language it contained: "Neither slavery nor involuntary servitude, except as a punishment for crime . . . shall exist within the United States." As he could see, the official notice boasted the signatures of both the Speaker of the House and the vice president of the United States—the vice president acting in his capacity as president of the U.S. Senate. Almost by instinct, Lincoln seized a pen and added his own signature as well, writing in a bold script: "Approved, February 1. 1865. Abraham Lincoln." Perhaps he failed to realize that presidents were not required to sign resolutions on constitutional amendments. Maybe he simply wanted to add his autograph to those of the others. Either way, he was not about to be left out of this great moment—or this priceless document. He had fought too hard for its passage. His name belonged on it, too. Whether or not he was required—or entitled—to approve it, he signed his name.

A few hours later, a band of musicians gathered outside on the White House lawn and began to serenade the president. The mood was joyful. Defying the winter cold, exuberant citizens joined the throng and began shouting for Lincoln to appear. Before long, the big windows on the second floor of the mansion opened wide, and the tall, thin figure of Lincoln, dressed, as always, in black, appeared in the moonlight. Not even his broad smile could disguise his tragic appearance. He looked more tired than ever. His once-thick beard was shaved back into a scraggly cluster of whiskers on his chin. Great black circles ringed his sad eyes. A few strands of gray flecked his black hair. When the cheering subsided, the president began slowly speaking to the crowd in a loud voice. Microphones had not yet been invented. He had no written text; he spoke from the heart. Lincoln thanked the audience for its compliments, but insisted that tonight's occasion called for congratulations not to him alone, but "to the country and the whole world."

The Thirteenth Amendment, he declared, had been desperately needed. Passage meant that another terrible "disturbance"— another bloody civil war—would never again tear the country apart over the issue of slavery. Yes, he was also proud of his Emancipation Proclamation, now two years old. The proclamation had begun the important work of ending slavery, but it had not gone far enough. It applied only to states fighting a war against the Union, and not to loyal Southern states like Kentucky, Lincoln's own birth state—the "place of my nativity," he called it. There, slavery still existed, protected by the original Constitution. Even in the Confederacy, the proclamation had freed only those slaves in areas the Union Army had captured over the past two years. And it did not apply to the children of those slaves. As Lincoln put it, the proclamation alone simply could not outlaw slavery everywhere, but the amendment would. It was, in Lincoln's words, "a King's cure for all the evils." To another hearty round of loud applause, he declared, "It winds the whole thing up." It was a "great moral victory."

Within a few days, however, it became clear that it was a great victory that Congress did not particularly want to share with the president. On February 7, the U.S. Senate actually passed yet another resolution complaining that Lincoln's approval had been "unnecessary." As one irritated senator explained, presidents simply had "nothing to do" with amendments to the Constitution. Their signatures were not required, and Lincoln's was not appreciated. Worst of all, the criticism had come from the lips of a senator from Lincoln's own home state, Illinois. In fact, the man who offered these ungracious remarks had defeated Lincoln himself for the Senate ten years earlier.

If this latest vote upset Lincoln, he did not allow it to show. By then, Illinois had done something far more important. It had become the first state in the Union to approve the Thirteenth Amendment. Just hours after Congress voted, Illinois had voted, too.

Within weeks, as other states rushed to approve it as well, the Thirteenth Amendment became much more than a resolution adopted by Congress. It became a precious object, copies of which ordinary Americans could purchase to display at home. Artists began producing pictures of the actual resolution, complete with portraits of all the congressmen and senators who had voted for it. Lincoln's picture almost always appeared at the very top. And, legal or not, his signature usually appeared on the bottom, just where he had written it out in ink on February 1. From then on, and for all time to come, the name Abraham Lincoln would be associated with the amendment that, once and for all, did away with what some people called America's original sin: slavery. Once it was ratified, four million enslaved people were forever free. Sadly, when the required number of states approved the amendment ten months later, Lincoln was already dead.

By then, no extra vote in Congress, no petty complaining, could ever separate Abraham Lincoln's name from this grand achievement.

It had been a long time coming. Lincoln had hated slavery from his earliest days. But not until the last few months of his life did he summon the boldness and political genius to strike the blow that legally killed it. The road to freedom proved long, bumpy, and uneven—rutted with detours, obstacles, and frustrating delays. It took most of his lifetime for Lincoln himself to overcome the prejudices he grew up with, and to discard the caution that always marked his leadership style. But when he did, he not only grew and changed; he helped America grow and change as well.

*   *   *

CHAPTER ONE

THE MAKING OF A LIBERATOR

I have always thought that all men should be free," Abraham Lincoln proudly remembered near the end of his eventful life. Then he joked, "Whenever I hear any one arguing for slavery I feel a strong impulse to see it tried on him personally." By then, the Thirteenth Amendment was well on its way to being ratified by the states. And Lincoln was already known as the Great Emancipator. But even earlier, Lincoln had declared: "If slavery is not wrong, nothing is wrong. I can not remember when I did not so think, and feel."

Lincoln himself had been born in 1809 in the state of Kentucky, a place where slavery was perfectly legal and widely accepted. His father was a poor farmer. Thomas Lincoln never had enough money to afford slaves of his own to work on his land, but even if he had been wealthier, he might never have agreed to do so. Thomas was a religious man and did not believe God gave any human being the right to own another. He thought slavery was also unfair to poor white people who were forced to till their own soil without the help of slave labor. It was said there were no more than fifty slaves in the entire Kentucky county where the Lincolns lived, but Thomas objected anyway. In 1816, when Abe was seven, Thomas moved his family northwest to the state of Indiana, mostly in search of better land and more opportunity, but perhaps to get farther away from slavery as well.

Young Abe grew up in Indiana without seeing much of school-rooms. "I could hardly read or write," he remembered. "My education had been sadly neglected." He did not see much of slavery either. Coming of age in Indiana, Lincoln seldom glimpsed any black people at all, slave *or* free. Meanwhile, his father continued to struggle to make ends meet. Often, when the family needed extra money, Thomas hired Abe out to his neighbors for a fee—and, as the law dictated, collected all of Abe's salary for himself. Abe did not get to keep a penny of the money he earned with his own sweat: he was something like a slave himself. And he was very much in demand. By the time he was a teenager, Abe was already more than six feet tall and so strong he could chop down trees, split log rails, and build wooden fences faster than most grown men. Most of the farmers who hired Abe liked him very much. He told funny stories and excelled at sports like wrestling. But the farmers also noticed that when they weren't watching him closely, Abe often put his axe down and headed for the nearest tree to sit in the shade and read. His nose always seemed to be buried in a book.

When Abe's mother, Nancy, died in 1818, Thomas found a new wife and brought her back to the family cabin to help raise Abe and his sister, Sarah. Sarah Bush Johnston Lincoln brought along children of her own, some furniture that seemed far better

Young Lincoln was an expert rail-splitter, and his father often hired him out to neighbors to chop down trees and build log fences. But Abe was so poor he probably never wore the kind of spruce outfit shown in this painting by J. L. G. Ferris (Courtesy Library of Congress)

than any Abe had ever seen, and most important of all, books. Reading them by firelight, or whenever his father allowed him time from his chores to study, his back propped up against an upside-down chair, Abe devoured every book he could get his hands on. As he grew older he read newspapers, too. His stepmother, Sarah, who encouraged him, turned out to be one of the most important people in the future president's entire life. Had she not insisted that Thomas give the boy as much time as possible to read, he might have ended up a poor farmer like his father, who could, Abe remembered, only "bunglingly" sign his own name.

Around the age of fifteen Abe scribbled his first lines of poetry in a large book. Whether he copied them for another book or invented them himself is not known. However, his neighbors noted that he enjoyed making up rhymes, usually to tease the local preacher. Certainly the verses reveal their author already to be a talented, humorous young man with his eye on the future:

> Abraham Lincoln
> his hand and pen
> he will be good but
> god knows When . . .

> Abraham Lincoln is my nam[e]
> And with my pen I wrote the same
> I wrote it in both hast[e] and speed
> and left it here for fools to read

Young Abe read the entire Bible, including the Old Testament story of the Jewish people's escape from slavery in Egypt. It made a strong impression on him. He also enjoyed poetry, Aesop's Fables, and an especially popular book of the day about the life of George Washington. The Washington book he borrowed from one of his neighbors, and loved it so much he took it to bed with him in the small loft where he slept in the family cabin, right beneath the roofline. One night it rained so hard that water leaked into the ceiling and soaked the old book. Its pages swelled with water. Lincoln apologized to its owner, who made him work in his fields until the ruined volume was paid for. Lincoln hated the chores he had to do, but never forgot the incident—or the book. He loved its chapters about the battlefields, heroes, and "hardships" of the Revolution. But these stories also set him to thinking, "boy even though I was," that there was something special that these soldiers fought for, "something that held out a great promise to all the people of the world to all time to come." And that was the promise in the Declaration of Independence that all men were created equal and shared the same right to "life, liberty, and the pursuit of happiness." The idea would never leave him.

When he was twenty-two, Abe and his family packed up and moved yet again, this time to the state of Illinois. There, he helped his father clear new land for planting and chopped wood to build a new log cabin home. He was an adult now, and it was time to strike out on his own. After a terrible winter, he finally said his good-byes and headed off on foot to begin life away from his family. He settled in a small Illinois village alongside a shallow river: the town of New Salem.

Few black people lived in the vicinity of his new hometown. Out of twelve thousand settlers in the county, only thirty-eight were black, and two-thirds of those were free people of color. But Lincoln came face to face with slavery soon enough. Abe had earlier joined a group of friends on an adventure to the Deep South. Their plan was to float some cargo on a wooden flatboat down the Mississippi River all the way to New Orleans. Along

the way, their raft came under attack one night by a group of
seven black men who meant to rob them. Lincoln and his com-
panions fought them off, but not before a knife or some other
weapon sliced into Abe's thumb. Lincoln bore a scar from the
battle for the rest of his life, but never blamed all people of color
for the experience, nor did it stop him and his friends from
taking a second flatboat of goods down the Mississippi soon
after.

The sight of New Orleans—the "Crescent City," as it was
known—must have dazzled him. Lincoln had never seen such
a big place. New Orleans was filled with handsome wooden
homes, restaurants, hotels, churches, and exotic people who spoke
French as well as English. But something else was different here:
the streets were crowded with black people, and not all of them
walked the streets freely. Many were slaves. Some were actually
marched along together in chains. And worst of all, some were
sold in the streets at slave markets or auctions, sometimes offered to the highest bidder like cattle. Many of these people had
just been separated from mates, children, brothers, and sisters
without giving their consent. But their sorrow did not matter to
either their masters or the slave traders, for enslaved black people
had no rights at all. The male slaves who looked strongest, and
the women who looked as if they could bear the most children,
went for the highest prices. The white people who gathered to
bid on them poked at the slaves, or opened their mouths to check
their teeth. They treated these human beings like animals. If the
slaves objected, they were ignored or whipped.

Lincoln visited the slave market one day during his New Orleans visit and looked on in horror as a young girl was dragged

to the platform to be auctioned off. Abe's cousin remembered: "There it was we saw Negroes Chained—maltreated—whipt and scourged. I can say knowingly it was on this trip that he formed his opinion on slavery; it ran its iron in him then & there." Supposedly, Abe turned to his friends in a fury and said: "By God, boys, let's get away from this. If I ever get a chance to hit that thing"—by which he meant slavery—"I'll hit it hard." It was later proven that this "witness" was not even traveling with Lincoln on that voyage to Louisiana. But there is no doubt that Lincoln did observe slaves being sold on the New Orleans streets, and did find the sight sickening. Others agreed that he was so upset he could barely speak. He later sadly recounted the experience to friends back home in Illinois. The horrific sight of human beings shackled together and sold as property may have changed Lincoln's life—and eventually the nation's life—forever.

When young Lincoln returned to New Salem, his first priority was to decide on a career. So far, he admitted, he had been nothing more than a "piece of floating driftwood." He needed to choose a career and earn a steady income. He thought for a while about becoming a blacksmith; that job required great strength, and Lincoln had it to spare. But a life of physical labor was not for him. He knew enough about such work, he joked, to know he did not love it. Instead, Lincoln worked for a time in the local post office and then tried his hand at surveying. Later he opened a grocery store. But it "winked out," as he described its failure, saddling him with a large debt that took him years to pay off. Despite these crushing disappointments he continued to read. He studied grammar and memorized the poems of Robert Burns and monologues from the plays of William Shakespeare.

He started reading newspapers and grew especially interested in politics. He became friends with neighbors who lent him still more books and encouraged him to better himself.

Lincoln soon found his true calling. He was extremely popular and cared about his community and neighbors. He wanted to better their lives—to give them a fair chance, just as the Declaration of Independence had promised everyone. So he decided to become a politician and run for a seat in the Illinois State Assembly. While doing so he began to study law, too. In those days, most law students read the required legal books on their own without the help of teachers or formal classes. Only a handful of them went to an actual law school. Lincoln taught himself to be a lawyer entirely on his own.

His first campaign for political office was interrupted, however, when an Indian chief named Black Hawk marched five hundred Sac and Fox warriors into Illinois in 1832, breaking the terms of a recent treaty. Like many excited young men in his neighborhood, Lincoln quickly joined the local militia and marched off to defend the state. Lincoln's own grandfather—also named Abraham Lincoln—had been murdered by Indians years earlier in Kentucky. It is likely that Abe remembered the stories of his violent death when he decided to enlist.

Although Lincoln had no military experience at all, to his "surprize," as he put it, his fellow soldiers elected him as their company captain. This honor delighted Lincoln. It was a "success," he said, "which gave me more pleasure than any I have had since." Still, Lincoln and his men never saw much action during the Black Hawk War. "Yes sir," he later joked, "in the days of the Black Hawk war, I fought, bled, and came away." He never saw any "live, fighting indians," he joked, "but I had a good many bloody struggles against the mosquitoes." Lincoln rather liked military life. Most of the time the soldiers did little more than idle away their time in a "sitting or horizontal posture," one fellow volunteer recalled. They had no battles, but plenty of "plays and songs." Lincoln especially enjoyed the athletic contests with both "red boys and white." He rarely lost a wrestling match or a swimming race.

When their term of service came to an end, most of his friends returned home. But Lincoln signed up several more times, even though he once again became only a private and the war cost him time needed to campaign for the state assembly. By the time Chief Black Hawk called off his invasion, ending the war, Lincoln had only a short time left before Election Day. In the end, the town of New Salem awarded their popular neighbor almost all of its votes. But few people in the rest of the district knew him yet, and Lincoln lost the election. It was the first and only time, he would remember, that he was ever "beaten by the people."

Actually, the war had brought out something important in Lincoln's character: his respect for all people, regardless of race. One night, the soldiers in his outfit were awakened from their sleep when an elderly Indian innocently approached their campfire. The poor old man was hungry and desperate to get something to eat. But the soldiers were so bored by the lack of action during the so-called war that they began shouting that they should execute the Indian. It was Lincoln who came to the frightened man's rescue. He announced to the soldiers that if they wanted to harm the old man they would have to get through him first. Lincoln was already known as the strongest soldier in camp and the best wrestler. The gang cooled down and backed off. Thanks to Lincoln, they did the elderly man no harm. Instead they fed their starving visitor and sent him on his way.

When he returned home to stay, Lincoln successfully earned his law license and on his second try for office won a seat in the Illinois Assembly. In the capital city of Vandalia, Lincoln began to work closely with other members of his political party—the Whigs—introducing laws to build roads, bridges, and canals to connect the rural state. Though his clothes looked shoddy and his appearance seemed odd, the awkward freshman assemblyman quickly made a tremendous impression on his better-educated, better-dressed colleagues. He enjoyed life in the capital, but he was lonely. He had earlier developed a serious crush on a pretty New Salem girl named Ann Rutledge, daughter of the local innkeeper. Not everyone agrees about whether their friendship ever blossomed into a true love affair. Ann was engaged to another man, who had headed off to New York State to conduct some business before their marriage. He never returned. Lincoln was shy with women and might have felt comfortable only with a girl who was already "promised" to another man. The relationship came with no pressure. But then young Ann suddenly took sick and died. Lincoln grew so despondent he nearly had a nervous breakdown. He could not get Ann out of his mind. He spent endless hours weeping at her fresh grave, worrying about how she might feel when it rained. Friends thought he would never recover from his loss. Only after a long period of mourning was Lincoln able to resume his life and work.

A few years later, his friends introduced him to an older woman named Mary Owens. By all accounts, she was overweight and missing a few teeth. But she was educated, lively, and had money of her own. Lincoln hinted he would ask to marry her providing she assured him first that she would accept. Mary hinted she would indeed consent, but only if Lincoln asked first. The situation seemed hopeless. Eventually, Mary left New Salem altogether, but the two agreed to keep exchanging letters about their future. Lincoln was not very romantic. In 1837, he wrote to warn Mary that if she married him, she "would have to be poor without the means of hiding your poverty." As Lincoln expressed it, "Whatever woman may cast her lot with mine, should any ever do so, it is my intention to do all in my power to make her happy." But, he advised: "My opinion is that you had better not do it. You have not been accustomed to hardship, and it may be more severe than you now imagine." That was enough for Mary. She turned him down.

"I was really a little in love with her," Lincoln later admitted. But Mary Owens claimed that "Mr. Lincoln was deficient in those little links which make up the chain of woman's happiness—at least it was so in my case." Even after Lincoln became president, she never regretted saying no to his halfhearted proposal. His feelings hurt, Lincoln said some unkind things about Mary—rare for him—and concluded "never again to think of marrying." As he joked, "I can never be satisfied with anyone who would be block-head enough to have me." But it was clear he was disappointed. Believing he would never have much of a personal life, he went back to work in Vandalia.

He fared much better in his public life than in his private life. Abraham Lincoln's finest moment as a young state legislator came in March 1837, when he signed his name to a protest against slavery. Most Americans—including those living in free states like Illinois—continued to be silent about the slavery issue in those days. Even the protest that Lincoln wrote with a fellow assemblyman named Dan Stone admitted that the U.S. Congress had "no power, under the constitution, to interfere with the institution of slavery in the different States." But Lincoln and Stone were outraged that the Illinois legislature had just passed a resolution disapproving of "abolition societies"—groups devoted to ending slavery. Many people of the time considered these organizations radical and dangerous. "Abolitionists"—the name given to people who wanted slavery abolished immediately— were often attacked, and some were murdered. Most Americans still considered them to be extremists.

Lincoln was no abolitionist—not yet, anyway—but he believed that the Illinois resolution missed a very important point: that slavery was morally wrong. So Lincoln voted against it. When it passed anyway, he wrote his statement of protest. The protest declared slavery to be both "injustice and bad policy." It was his first public statement about the institution he would later destroy. But he would say nothing more about slavery for years to come.

That year, Lincoln did cast one other important vote: to move the state capital to a new city, Springfield. He quickly decided to make the fast-growing town his own permanent home as well. On April 15, 1837, he packed his belongings into a couple of saddlebags and rode on horseback from New Salem to the new capital. Once there, he simply walked into the room of an acquaintance named Joshua Speed and asked if he could share his living space with him. Speed was agreeable, even though there would be only one bed for the both of them. "Well, Speed," Lincoln said, dropping his few possessions onto the floor, "I am moved."

Abraham Lincoln was twenty-eight years old. As it happened, it was the midpoint of his life. He had exactly twenty-eight more years to live—to the day.

CHAPTER TWO

ROMANCE, LAW, AND POLITICS

In Springfield, Lincoln's reputation as an attorney and politician grew steadily. He found work as a junior partner in a law firm and became particularly adept at trial work. Juries loved his droll stories and deft arguments, and often decided in favor of Lincoln's clients even if the law was not on their side. Meanwhile he continued to serve in the state legislature and began impressing audiences throughout the region with his talents as a public speaker. But Lincoln complained that social life in Springfield was "a dull business," admitting: "I am quite as lonesome here as ever I was anywhere in my life. I have been spoken to by but one woman since I've been here, and should not have been by her if she could have avoided it." Romance finally arrived after two years in town.

In around 1839, he met another Mary—a sparkling young woman named Mary Ann Todd, a cousin of his first law partner John Todd Stuart. She had just moved to Springfield to live with her married sister, Elizabeth Todd Edwards. Mary's one and only goal was to find a husband, as she was already over twenty when she arrived—practically an old maid by the standards of the early nineteenth century! The Illinois capital was filled with eligible bachelors, and Mary was pretty and flirtatious enough to soon enjoy her choice of beaus. She was wildly popular at local parties and had men fluttering around her seeking her attention.

One of these suitors was an up-and-coming politician named Stephen A. Douglas, who was in many ways the complete opposite of Abraham Lincoln. Appropriately, one became known as the "Little Giant," the other as "Long Abe." Douglas, the "Little Giant," was as short as Lincoln was tall, as boastful as Lincoln was modest, and loved to smoke, eat, and drink more than was good for him. His neighbors already knew that Lincoln never used tobacco and never consumed liquor or wine. Rather than brag, Lincoln usually poked fun at his own homely appearance. From the first, the two rivals opposed each other in politics, too. Douglas was a Democrat. He worshipped former President Andrew Jackson and did not believe in big banks or government spending to build new roads. He believed such projects required higher taxes, which his supporters could ill afford to pay. Lincoln, on the other hand, was an enthusiastic member of the Whig Party. He supported road and canal projects that would link the state more closely and make it easier to ship goods from town to town. He favored a strong banking system that made certain that money remained in good supply. The issue of slavery had not yet divided Lincoln and Douglas, though eventually it would.

Mary probably could have married the dynamic Stephen Douglas. He was certainly the more famous and successful of the two. She later boasted that he indeed became one of her ad-mirers. But instead, she set her sights on Lincoln, homely and awkward though he was. She saw something in him from the start that many others failed to recognize: a promise of future greatness. As she later said with pride, she may have had many suitors, but Lincoln was "a world above them all." Yet theirs did not seem a natural match at the start of their friendship. It was said that Lincoln approached Mary at a party one evening and shyly declared, "Miss Todd, I want to dance with you in the worst way." As she later remembered, that was exactly the way he danced—in the worst way. But before long, Abraham and Mary were deeply in love and "courting" at Mary's sister's home. Abra-ham proposed, and Mary accepted, but something happened be-fore the wedding they planned for January 1, 1841. Most likely, the groom got cold feet and backed out. Whoever was at fault, both took the breakup hard. Humiliated, Mary remained se-cluded at her sister's house and refused for a time to see anyone. Lincoln became so depressed that friends feared he would take his own life. He was miserable, he said, mostly because he had wounded Mary's feelings. He felt he could not live with her, but could not live without her, either. Abraham consoled himself by heading off to visit his onetime Springfield roommate, Josh Speed, at his family home near Louisville, Kentucky. There, Lin-coln relaxed in comfort, waited on day and night by the Speed family's African American slaves. If Lincoln felt any discomfort or guilt over the existence of slavery at the Speed plantation, he never said so.

On his way home, accompanied by Speed on a steamboat to St. Louis, he witnessed a scene that disturbed him deeply—and haunted him for the rest of his life. He had just boarded the canal boat when he glimpsed a group of slaves on deck. To Lincoln's horror, they were chained together. Yet they seemed incredibly happy, sang songs, and "cracked jokes," he recalled. But surely, Lincoln thought, they knew they had been taken away from their friends and family and were about to be sold in the South. "They were chained six and six together," Lincoln vividly remembered. "A small iron clevis"—a U-shaped iron horseshoe with holes in it through which chains could be strung—"was around the left wrist of each, and this fastened to the main chain by a shorter one at a convenient distance from, the others; so that the negroes were strung together precisely like so many fish upon a trot-line. In this condition they were being separated forever from the scenes of their childhood, their friends, their fathers and mothers, and brothers and sisters, and many of them, from their wives and children, and going into perpetual slavery where the lash of the master is proverbially more ruthless and unrelenting than any other where." For years, he could not get the sight out of his mind.

By then, millions of slaves were held in equally cruel bondage throughout the South, with no right to remain with their loved ones if their owners chose to separate and sell them. Much of the region was devoted to farming, and the largest farms—which were called "plantations"—grew acre after acre of cotton, rice, or tobacco, which required huge numbers of workers to plant and harvest, often in suffocating heat. The first slaves had arrived in Virginia in the early 1600s. Over the centuries, hundreds of thousands of black children had been born into slavery and continued to work on the plantations. Tens of thousands more were captured in Africa and brought to America against their will aboard slave ships so fearfully crowded and filthy that many died before they arrived. If they lived, they were forced to work for no pay for the rest of their lives. They could not learn to read or formally get married. And if they had children, their sons and daughters became the property of their white masters for the rest of *their* lives—and, moreover, could be taken from their parents at any time and sold away.

In the North, where the climate was cooler than the South's and the farms smaller, most people tended their crops themselves or with their families. Slavery disappeared in most Northern states by the 1840s, and its economy grew more diverse under a dynamic system that depended on free labor. Lincoln never suggested that Southerners were more evil than Northerners for supporting slavery. In fact, he often admitted that if their geography had been reversed—had Northerners lived in the South and Southerners in the North—they would have reversed their views on the slavery issue, too. That did not mean Lincoln thought slavery a good thing. He passionately believed in the free labor system—in the right of every worker to do well enough to eventually be able to work for himself, perhaps even to employ others. As he put it, "Free labor has the inspiration of hope; pure slavery has no hope." On this subject, Lincoln and his former fiancée agreed: slavery was an evil, but it would be difficult to dislodge it from a region where it had so long existed. The rights and feelings of the slaves themselves were seldom part of the discussion, at least among the vast majority of white people. Slaves were considered property, and no property in the entire South was worth more than its millions of enslaved people. When

Abraham and Mary first met, slavery no longer existed in Illinois. But the few black people who lived in Springfield worked as servants or laborers. They enjoyed few opportunities even in a supposedly free city.

Abraham and Mary did not get back together for nearly a year and a half. A local newspaper editor and his wife finally encouraged them to start courting again at their house, away from the suspicious gaze of Mary's sister, who did not approve of Lincoln. There the two renewed their friendship and rediscovered how much they had in common. They certainly shared a bond, because both had lost their mothers at an early age. Mary might have been livelier and more sociable than Abraham, but both of them loved books, poetry, and ideas. Most of all, they shared a passion for politics. Mary was a Whig, too. In fact, her father, Robert S. Todd, was a rather famous Whig back home in Lexington, Kentucky. Mr. Todd was even friends with the great Kentucky senator Henry Clay, and that may have been enough to sway Lincoln. Clay was his hero.

But even after their long separation, the two lovers remained very different, too. Mary was fiery and unpredictable—quick to laugh but easy to anger. Abraham was slow and steady, and sometimes seemed to be daydreaming. He could read for hours without even glancing up from his book or newspaper, ignoring everyone and everything around him. Mary, on the other hand, needed constant attention. Most significantly of all, though they both originally hailed from the same state of Kentucky, they had been raised in very different circumstances. Lincoln grew up in a primitive log cabin deep in the prairie; Mary grew up in a fine home in a city. Mary's family was wealthy, while Abraham's was poverty-stricken. Mary's father sent her to college. Lincoln's father allowed his son less than a year of actual schooling during his entire childhood.

Perhaps the biggest difference between them was their personal childhood experience with slavery. Lincoln's father was too poor to afford slaves and disapproved of slavery on moral grounds, anyway. But Mary's father did own slaves. In fact, Mary Todd was raised by an African American house servant she called "Mammy Sally." They grew especially close after Mary's mother died. However, Mammy Sally was more than a servant; she was also something of a freedom fighter, risking her life to help other slaves escape through Lexington, even though if she had been discovered, she might have been severely punished. Little Mary learned from Sally to sing the hymn, "Hide Me O My Savior"—a prayer for escaping slaves—and may have watched as Sally left coded messages for escaping slaves in the form of kerchiefs or bandanas strung along the front fence of the Todd home. Mammy Sally may have inspired the young girl to think harder about what freedom meant, although for many years, Mary would not think of African Americans as equals. But from an early age she knew how brutal slave life could be. Mary no doubt saw many slaves beaten at the town whipping post and heard stories about the many local people who viciously mistreated their slaves. Even her father came to hate slavery. But not enough to free his own slaves.

Eventually it was the subject of politics that brought Abraham and Mary back together. They both ardently favored the Whig Party and both disliked slavery, even if neither yet knew quite what to do about it. And it was one particular political crisis that finally inspired Abraham to take the leap where marriage was concerned. He had been writing a series of extremely sarcastic articles for the town newspaper, poking fun at a local Irish American Democrat named James Shields. The articles were extremely hurtful, but in those days politicians often attacked each other personally, and Lincoln was no exception. After one such assault, Mary decided she wanted to get in on the exciting action, too. So she wrote and published a poem that ridiculed Shields just as cruelly, making particular sport of his Irish heritage. Outraged, Shields demanded to know who wrote the rhymes. Lincoln valiantly took the blame to protect Mary, and Shields demanded an apology. When Lincoln refused, Shields challenged him to a duel. Cooler heads eventually prevailed and the fight was called off at the last minute, but Mary was deeply impressed by Lincoln's gallant behavior. Just a few weeks later, on November 1, 1842, the two married in the parlor of Mary's sister's home. Politics had united two wildly different personalities and turned them into a single-minded couple for life. Now both would devote their time to the same goal: making Abraham Lincoln a success.

For the rest of their lives, they never spoke of the near-duel again. In any event, much bigger battles awaited them in the future.

*   *   *

CHAPTER THREE

THE LINCOLNS GO TO WASHINGTON

In 1846, the voters of Springfield and the surrounding community elected Lincoln to serve in Congress. By now the Lincolns had two small sons, Robert and Eddy. When it came time to leave for Washington, D.C., the entire family headed off to the nation's capital together. On their way, they stopped to visit Mary's father and stepmother. There they accepted without complaint the service of the Todd family's slaves. The Lincolns still had no violent objections to slavery, at least as practiced by people living in the South.

They found Washington itself to be a Southern city. Slaves could be seen everywhere, toiling away for many of the congressmen and senators at their homes, and working around town as laborers, waiters, and drivers. When local slaves tried on one famous occasion to escape by smuggling themselves on a ship docked in the river, owners learned of their daring plan and recaptured them. Then the slave owners complained bitterly that antislavery congressmen were at fault for repeatedly

LEFT: *The earliest known photograph of Lincoln—taken in 1846 in his Springfield, Illinois hometown, shortly after his election to his one and only term in Congress. (Daguerreotype by Nicholas H. Shepherd, courtesy Library of Congress)*

RIGHT: *Lincoln's wife, Mary Todd Lincoln, probably posed for this daguerreotype the same day as Lincoln posed for his. Much shorter than her husband, Mary never allowed the couple to be photographed together. (Daguerreotype by Nicholas H. Shepherd, courtesy Library of Congress)*

making speeches suggesting that black freedom was possible. Some of the angriest citizens formed a mob and marched on a local newspaper that supported the abolition of slavery. They nearly burned the office down.

Taking up his post in December 1847, Lincoln met many congressmen willing to fight to protect slavery. From the windows of the Capitol building, he could see a horrific slave prison that had operated for fifty years along the street just below. It was "a sort of negro livery stable," he remembered with distaste, "where droves of negroes were collected, temporarily kept, and finally taken to Southern markets." Lincoln was disgusted to see human beings treated "precisely like droves of horses." But there was nothing he could do about the situation. These vile slave pens were perfectly legal. As much as they detested slavery, Lincoln and his wife made no secret of their affection for Washington's minstrel shows, at which white people blackened their faces and imitated people of color in grotesque songs and dances. It was a different age, and the way blacks and whites regarded each other remained a complicated matter.

But there was almost no escaping the horrors of slavery in Washington—even at home. The Lincolns lived in a boarding-house across the road from the Capitol. Many of the residents there were fellow Whigs. Most disliked slavery. But one day, while Lincoln was away at work, a white man came to the door to arrest one of the free black waiters working at the house. It seemed that the waiter had been regularly sending money to buy his freedom, but had fallen short by just sixty dollars. That was enough to force him back into slavery. After a violent struggle that horrified the residents, Mary included, the dazed man was shackled and dragged back to captivity. None of the boarders had the legal right or moral courage to lift a finger to help him.

Congress, however, was beginning to wake up to the evils of slavery—at least such could be said for its Northern members. The Mexican War was ending with a great victory for the United States. With peace, however, came the addition of vast new Southern territory, including Texas, and proslavery senators were eager to make sure slave ownership would be permitted there. It was not just that they wanted slavery itself to spread. If slave owners moved into these new regions, they would be likely to elect still more proslavery senators and representatives. The so-called "slave power" in Congress would thus increase further, and slavery would remain legal for decades to come.

Whigs like Lincoln objected. A Pennsylvania congressman named David Wilmot introduced a bill that would ban slavery from all the new territory acquired from Mexico. Lincoln later estimated that he voted for Wilmot's proposal dozens of times. But it never passed. There was still no strong or united sentiment in Washington to outlaw slavery or prevent it from spreading. In fact, for a long time, Congress was not even allowed to debate the issue of slavery. From 1836 to 1844, a so-called "gag rule" prevented the subject from ever coming up for a discussion, much less a vote.

In 1849, Lincoln decided to do something on his own to combat slavery. Though he was only a first-term congressman and had very little power or influence in the House of Representatives, he proposed a law that would end slavery throughout Washington, D.C. Like many Whigs, Lincoln believed that the existence of slavery in the national capital was a national disgrace.

Still, Lincoln's idea was quite conservative. It promised that slave owners in the city would first have a chance to vote on approval of the measure. It required that the children of slaves be made to work as apprentices. Many of his fellow Whigs thought Lincoln's proposal did not go far enough. But it apparently went *too* far for many of his other colleagues. Congress refused to consider the law, and slavery remained legal in the city for the next thirteen years. But at least Lincoln had tried.

Abraham Lincoln's career in Congress ended after just one term (1847–1849). He had agreed in advance to let another Whig politician run for his seat next time. Much as he yearned to stand for reelection, he kept his promise to bow out. Believing his life in politics was over, Lincoln headed home to Springfield and resumed his life as a lawyer. He was certain the people would never call on him to serve in high political office again. Even worse news followed. In 1850, after a long illness, the Lincolns' sprightly two-year-old son Eddy took sick and died, devastating his mother and father. Mary was soon pregnant again, but they remained in mourning for their lost second child for years.

Lincoln's family and political life remained gloomy, but his legal business began to flourish. Typically, Lincoln and his fellow lawyers traveled together from town to town, signing up and representing clients whenever and wherever local courts went into session. They were not choosy about who paid for their services. To the surprise of some, for example, in October 1847, just before he left to take up his duties in Washington, Lincoln served as a lawyer for a client named Robert Matson. Matson was seeking to prevent his slaves from going free while they were working for him in the free state of Illinois. Lincoln argued that the workers were not residents of Illinois, and thus technically remained in slavery. Illinois had passed a law four years earlier allowing masters to take their slaves into free territory for what were called "sojourns"—or temporary work. Pennsylvania allowed slaves to "sojourn" there for up to six months; New York for nine. In the Matson case, the judge ruled otherwise, and set the slaves free. Some people, then and since, have criticized Lincoln for taking the case. But as a professional attorney, he believed he had an obligation to defend people to the best of his ability. The Matson case provides yet another example of how long it took Lincoln to become a true antislavery man.

In these years, it was Stephen Douglas, then a U.S. senator, and not Abraham Lincoln, who achieved fame and success in Washington. Senator Douglas helped pass Henry Clay's Compromise of 1850, an attempt to cool down the increasingly heated national argument over slavery. The package of bills called for California to enter the Union as a free state. It banned the trading of slaves, but not slavery itself, in the nation's capital. But to achieve so-called "balance" between the opposing sides, it also introduced a tough new Fugitive Slave Act that required all Northerners to capture and return runaway slaves. For years, brave abolitionists had helped fugitive slaves escape through a system of secret safe houses known as the Underground Railroad. Throughout the North, opponents blasted the new law as the cruelest and most inhumane yet introduced in America. Many abolitionist whites and free blacks vowed to disobey it. The rising young African American leader Frederick Douglass, an escaped slave, urged fellow black men to resist the new law to the death. Lincoln disliked the law, too, but at the time saw no way to fight it. "I hate to see the poor creatures hunted down; and caught, and carried back to their stripes, and unrewarded toils," he said of the Fugitive Slave Act, "but I bite my lips and keep quiet."

Writing some time later to Josh Speed, who continued to support slavery, Lincoln was still vividly remembering the painful sight of the chained slaves they had once seen together on a steamboat. "You remember, as I well do, that from Louisville to the mouth of the Ohio [River], there were, on board, ten or a dozen slaves, shackled together with irons. That sight was a continual torment to me; and I see something like it every time I touch the Ohio, or any other slave border. It is not fair for you to assume, that I have no interest in a thing which has, and continually exercises the power of making me miserable. You ought rather to appreciate how much the great body of the Northern people do crucify their feelings, in order to maintain their loyalty to the constitution and the Union." To Lincoln, "Slave-breeders and slave-traders" were, in his words, "a small, odious, and detested class."

Not long afterward, Lincoln's great hero Henry Clay died. What Lincoln had admired most about Clay was his belief that the American Union—another term for the United States—should remain firmly together forever. The idea of the Union became almost holy to Lincoln. On July 6, 1852, he gave a long eulogy to the old senator at the state capitol building in Springfield. Retired or not, his neighbors still thought Lincoln the best public speaker in town, and the ideal man to pay tribute to the old Whig lion.

Although Clay himself had owned as many as sixty slaves, the politician known as the "Great Compromiser" had for years believed that enslaved people should be set free—but also returned to Africa, even if they had never lived there. Many other white people believed in this idea, too. It became known as "colonization," and it inspired supporters to form societies throughout the nation to argue for the idea of deporting black people. To modern ears, the idea sounds extremely racist. Even back then, a significant number of Americans thought it would be immoral, not to mention physically impossible, to gather up so many black people and ship them back across the ocean. Although most whites did not care what they thought or felt, African Americans of course believed they had every right to stay in this country. Free blacks argued that this wish should be respected by one and all, since their ancestors had certainly not asked white slave traders to capture them in Africa and bring them here against their will in the first place. Besides, their families had lived here on American soil for generations, even centuries. Many people of color could trace their American roots back many more generations than the country's hundreds of thousands of more recent German- and Irish-born immigrants.

Nonetheless, even humane men like Lincoln were attracted to the colonization idea. They thought colonization could convince Southerners to give up slavery by calming their fears that once they were free, blacks would punish them for their years of mistreatment by attacking them. Lincoln himself did not participate in Springfield's colonization society—he was never a joiner—but when he rose to offer his tribute to Henry Clay he surely had this so-called "solution" very much on his mind. Clay, he noted with admiration, had first proposed the idea as far back as 1816. He had stressed its "moral fitness" and believed that once slaves were freed and "transplanted in a foreign land, they will carry back to their native soil the rich fruits of civilization, law and liberty." To Lincoln, "Every succeeding year has added strength to the hope" that colonization could occur. "May it indeed be realized!" he proclaimed. It was time, he added, for "restoring a captive people to their long-lost father-land, with bright prospects for the future."

There can be little doubt about where Abraham Lincoln stood on the slavery issue at this time. He hated the idea of it. The thought of the cruelty of slavery haunted him. But at this time, only eight years before he ran for president, he was certainly not yet a great emancipator. He was more like a great colonizer. But he was not really yet great enough *himself* to accomplish much in *any* field. Where the subject of race was concerned, he still had a good deal to learn. And he soon would.

CHAPTER FOUR

THE PRAIRIES ARE ON FIRE

In 1854, when Congress finally acted again on slavery, the House and Senate voted not to kill or curtail it. They voted to allow it to spread. A new law made it possible for the settlers in the nation's new western territories—places like Kansas and Nebraska—to vote for themselves on whether or not to allow slavery to exist within their borders. This meant that the old Missouri Compromise, which since 1820 had prohibited slavery above the latitude of 36°30′ north, became null and void. The new law was the work of none other than Mary Lincoln's onetime admirer Stephen A. Douglas. Many politicians thought this was a good idea. After all, America was a democracy. Perhaps majority rule should decide the issue. They called the new system "popular sovereignty."

But others—like Lincoln—were infuriated. They argued that no one had the right to spread slavery outside the states where it already existed. They warned that the new law would eventually make slavery legal in every part of the nation. It would destroy

Lincoln holds an anti-slavery newspaper to the camera as he poses in Chicago in 1854, the year he announced his opposition to slavery expansion. (Photo by Polycarpus von Schneidau, courtesy Library of Congress)

the American system of free labor. Douglas's so-called Kansas–
Nebraska Act "aroused" Lincoln, as he put it, to reenter politics
after a five-year retirement. When he began speaking out again,
it was on one issue only: the duty of every American to stop the
spread of slavery.

"Slavery," Lincoln told one audience in a famous speech in
Peoria that year, "is founded in the selfishness of man's nature—
opposition to it is his love for justice." Then he made clear his
anger at those, like Douglas, who said they did not care one way
or the other about slavery:

> This *declared* indifference, but as I must think, covert *real*
> zeal for the spread of slavery, I can not but hate. I hate it
> because of the monstrous injustice of slavery itself. I hate
> it because it deprives our Republican example of its just
> influence in the world—enables the enemies of free insti-
> tutions . . . to taunt us as hypocrites—causes the real friends
> of freedom to doubt our sincerity; and especially because
> it forces so many really good men amongst ourselves into
> an open war with the very fundamental principles of civil
> liberty.

Lincoln's Peoria speech made clear his differences with Senator Douglas. "Equal justice to the South," he pointed out, meant
to Democrats like Douglas that if "you do not object to my taking my hog to Nebraska, therefore I must not object to you taking your slave. Now, I admit this is perfectly logical, if there is
no difference between hogs and negroes." To Lincoln, the difference between property and human beings was important. "In

our greedy chase to make profit of the negro," he warned, "let us beware, lest we 'cancel and tear to pieces' even the white man's charter of freedom."

With inspiring words like these, Lincoln quickly became one of the most outspoken antislavery leaders in the West. His stem-winding speeches, each of which lasted as long as two hours, drew thousands of spectators. He was still a moderate on the slavery issue, not ready yet to support immediate freedom. But at least he had begun interacting with people of color. His Haitian-born barber in Springfield, William de Fleurville, became not only the man who cut his hair but a legal client as well. Lincoln represented the successful businessman in many of his affairs.

Lincoln's loudest critics still accused him of favoring aboli-tion—of making slavery illegal immediately, and all at once. In truth, only a tiny fraction of white Americans of the day so be-lieved. And Lincoln was not yet one of them in the 1850s. Even so, by simply opposing the *spread* of slavery he angered many Southerners—and also infuriated many people in his own state of Illinois who had moved there from the South. He was grow-ing more popular, but certainly not with everyone. In fact, his political comeback stalled when he lost a contest for an Illinois seat in the U.S. Senate in 1855. Lincoln now found himself to be a man without a political party. The Whigs had become ir-relevant. The organization simply faded away. But antislavery former Whigs banded together with antislavery Democrats dis-gusted with their party's tendency to side with the South and formed a new political party. Lincoln soon joined them. He be-came a Republican.

Two years later, in 1857, the U.S. Supreme Court issued one of its most terrifying decisions. A slave named Dred Scott had sued for his freedom, arguing that when his Missouri masters took him from Missouri to the free states of Illinois and Wisconsin, he was no longer a slave. The justices, however, disagreed. Under Chief Justice Roger B. Taney, an elderly slave owner from Maryland, the nation's highest court ruled by a vote of seven-to-two that whites were entitled to own slaves anywhere in the United States, North or South. People of color, added the court, could never become American citizens. In the most shocking words in the decision, Taney wrote that black people were of an "inferior order" and had "no rights which the white man was bound to respect."

The Dred Scott decision appalled Abraham Lincoln. He complained that the ruling made human beings seem less than human before the law. He thought it an embarrassment to the entire country and an insult to the original promise of the Declaration of Independence. On a practical level, he feared it would mean that slave owners would now be free to take their slaves anywhere they chose. By now, Lincoln was speaking out against slavery everywhere he could. The Dred Scott decision inspired another round of orations, in which Lincoln first began suggesting that antislavery Americans might not really have to obey the Supreme Court ruling after all. Because the court's decision was not unanimous and was based on "assumed historical facts which were not really true," he said in a speech at Springfield on June 26, it would not be "disrespectful" to treat the issue as still "unsettled." Otherwise, he warned, the court's decision would mean not only that Dred Scott and his wife and daughters were legally "not human enough to have a [legal] hearing, even if they were free," but "that *all* persons" like Dred Scott were "rightfully slaves." Worse, it meant that "the bondage of the Negro" was "universal and eternal." The idea that the "sacred" Declaration of Independence did not apply to people of color, he said, was so contrary to what the nation's founders believed that if they were to "rise up from their graves, they could not at all recognize it."

Lincoln was not yet by any means prepared to argue for racial equality. In fact, he told a Springfield audience that year that there remained "a natural disgust in the minds of nearly all white people to the idea" of the races living together. He admitted that the overwhelming majority of whites did not want to "vote, and eat, and sleep, and marry with negroes!" But he strongly insisted that "the Declaration of Independence includes ALL men, black as well as white." This was considered to be advanced thinking in 1857. Lincoln maintained that he did not have to choose to have a black woman as either a slave or a wife. "I can just leave her alone," he declared. "In some respects she certainly is not my equal; but in her natural right to eat the bread she earns with her own hands without asking leave of any one else, she is my equal, and the equal of all others." Lincoln reminded all who would listen that if Senator Douglas and the Democrats had their way, slavery would spread to every state in the Union.

Unlike Douglas, Lincoln felt true sympathy for enslaved people. He was discouraged to see that "all the powers of earth seem rapidly combining" to increase the misery of individual slaves. Lincoln made people pay attention to his ideas by using language everyone could understand. Not every white voter knew what it was like to be a slave. So Lincoln reminded them that a slave was like a lifetime prisoner, and a slave owner was no better than a jailer. "They have him in his prison house," Lincoln pointed out. "They have closed the heavy iron doors upon him, and now they have him, as it were, bolted in with a lock of a hundred keys, which can never be unlocked."

In 1858, the Republican Party of Illinois chose Abraham Lincoln to run against Douglas for the U.S. Senate. By now, almost all voters in the state knew that the one and only issue in the campaign would be slavery—the combined weight of the controversial Kansas–Nebraska Act and the equally charged Dred Scott decision couldn't be ignored. What would the future of the country be under these new rulings by Congress and the Court? In accepting the nomination in June, Lincoln left no doubt where he believed the nation was heading: either to total freedom, or total slavery. Taking the podium at the state capitol building on a hot June evening, he began by quoting from the Bible, and then explained how the verse applied to the United States:

"A house divided against itself cannot stand." I believe this government cannot endure, permanently half *slave* and half *free*. I do not expect the Union to be *dissolved*—I do not expect the house to *fall*—but I do expect it will cease to be divided. It will become *all* one thing, or *all* the other. Either the *opponents* of slavery, will arrest the further spread of it, and place it where the public mind shall rest in the belief that it is in the course of ultimate extinction; or its *advocates* will push it forward, till it shall become alike lawful in *all* the States, *old* as well as *new*—*North* as well as *South*.

No one doubted what the candidates' positions were on the slavery issue. Douglas believed voters in new territories should have a right to vote to include or outlaw slavery themselves. Lincoln believed that they had no right to do so, and that slavery must not be allowed to spread further under any circumstances.

✷

Then Lincoln hit upon an ingenious idea to get the attention of undecided voters. He challenged Douglas to a series of public debates to argue over the issue again and again. The senator was cornered. He was far better known than his Republican opponent and had nothing to gain by sharing platforms with him at major political events. Yet in that day, the code of manhood required Douglas to accept. If he refused he would have been branded a coward. So Douglas reluctantly agreed to seven debates with Lincoln, and from August to October the two candidates argued over the slavery issue from the northern outposts of the state to the southern. Astonished by the overwhelming public interest in the debates, one New York reporter marveled: "The prairies are on fire!"

Lincoln and Douglas broke no new real ground on the slavery issue during their famous debates that summer and fall. Their opinions remained fixed, their opposition to each other's position unbreakable. But the Lincoln–Douglas debates turned into a huge public attraction anyway, well attended by tens of thousands of raucous spectators. Politics was so popular at the time that the debates brought people by horseback, boat, and train. Others walked miles on foot. Mary attended at least one of the debates, as did young Robert, wearing the uniform of a club called the Springfield cadets to the last debate.

The speeches by Lincoln and Douglas attracted much daily newspaper coverage, too, and were closely followed by readers not only in Illinois, but nationwide. For the first time, the newspapers hired stenographers to take down every word of the debates in shorthand. Their transcripts were then rushed off to Chicago, set in type, and printed in "just" a few days—a process so breathtakingly fast for the mid-nineteenth century that, relatively speaking, it approached the immediacy of the modern-day blog or tweet.

The debates themselves did not always bring out the best in either the two candidates or their audiences. Lincoln and Douglas attacked each other personally and each exaggerated his opponent's record. Lincoln accused Douglas of wanting slavery to spread nationwide (he did not), and Douglas accused Lincoln of favoring racial equality (*he* did not). Excited crowds often interrupted the speakers to shout encouragements or insults, or to laugh at Lincoln's jokes. Fistfights often broke out among Lincoln and Douglas fans in the back rows, where too much food and liquor sometimes made tempers flare.

As for the speakers, they were more often than not at their worst. Eager to make Lincoln appear to favor black equality, Douglas freely used the N-word and hysterically warned that electing the Republican would mean integration and intermarriage. To quiet fears that he secretly approved of racial equality, Lincoln opened the fourth debate at Charleston—not far from where his stepmother lived—with a particularly unattractive reminder that he was still very much a white supremacist. "I am not, nor ever have been, in favor of bringing about in any way the social and political equality of the white and black races— that I am not now nor ever have been in favor of making voters or jurors of negroes, nor of qualifying them to hold office, nor to intermarry with white people." He still believed that "there is a physical difference between the white and black races which I believe will forever forbid the two races living together on terms of social and political equality." In holding this insensitive view, Lincoln was no different from the overwhelming majority of white men of his time.

But then he made clear precisely what separated him from opponents like Douglas and the truly racist Democrats. "[T] here is no reason in the world why the negro is not entitled to all the rights enumerated in the Declaration of Independence—the right of life, liberty, and the pursuit of happiness. I hold that he is as much entitled to these as the whiter man." At their very first debate at the village of Ottawa, Lincoln used tough language to attack Senator Douglas for believing otherwise. "When he is saying that the negro has no share in the Declaration of Independence, he is going back to the year of our revolution, and . . . is muzzling the cannon that thunders its annual return. When he is saying, as he often does, that if any people want slavery they have a right to have it, he is . . . perverting the human soul and eradicating the light of reason and the love of liberty on the American continent."

To another audience, Lincoln made light of Douglas's charges that he favored racial equality. He admitted he might never marry a woman of color himself, but pointed out: "I have no objection to any one else doing so. If a white man wants to marry a negro woman, let him, do it—*if the negro woman can stand it.*"

Privately, Lincoln made his innermost feelings clear. "As I would not be a *slave*, so I would not be a *master*," he jotted down on a scrap of paper. "This expressed my idea of democracy. Whatever differs from this . . . is no democracy." Lincoln had always believed slavery was a "tyrant demon" that made life horrible for whites as well as blacks. The challenge was how to make more moderate and conservative voters understand its moral and political consequences.

On October 15, 1858, Abraham Lincoln and Stephen Douglas met for their seventh and final debate in the town square at Alton, a village nestled along the Mississippi—the river past which Lincoln had once steered a flatboat en route to the slaveholding South. Douglas's usually powerful deep voice sounded hoarse that day. He was exhausted from the months of speech-making. Lincoln had made just as many speeches as his opponent, but his high, clear voice sounded as strong as ever that day. Here the Republican choice for the Senate gave his most stirring explanation of why slavery was morally wrong—not only for America, but also for oppressed people the world over:

> That is the real issue. That is the issue that will continue in this country when these poor tongues of Judge Douglas and myself shall be silent. It is the eternal struggle between these two principles—right and wrong—throughout the world. They are the two principles that have stood face to face from the beginning of time; and will ever continue to struggle. The one is the common right of humanity and the other the divine right of kings. It is the same principle

in whatever shape it develops itself. It is the same spirit that says, "You work and toil and earn bread, and I'll eat it." No matter in what shape it comes, whether from the mouth of a king who seeks to bestride the people of his own nation and live by the fruit of their labor, or from one race of men as an apology for enslaving another race, it is the same tyrannical principle.

In the end, the debates were not enough to propel the anti-slavery Republicans to victory. Douglas defeated Lincoln after all. If people had voted directly for either of the two candidates, Lincoln might well have squeezed out a narrow win. But in those days, Lincoln and Douglas's names did not even appear on the Illinois ballot. Instead, voters elected state legislators who in turn chose senators themselves. In 1858, enough Democrats won election to the state legislature to ensure that Douglas would be chosen for another term in Washington, and he was.

Lincoln was initially crushed by the defeat, but soon bounced back, vowing that where the slavery issue was concerned, he would not give up. The slavery debate was just heating up. People still looked to him for leadership.

"For the future," Lincoln pledged to a friend, "my view is the fight must go on." And to another, he wrote: "The cause of civil liberty must not be surrendered at the end of *one*, or even a *hundred* defeats. Another explosion will soon come."

✳　✳　✳

CHAPTER FIVE

RIGHT MAKES MIGHT

The "explosion" came less than two years later—and Lincoln helped ignite it. In late 1859, a group of young Republicans in New York City invited Lincoln to speak at a famous antislavery church in Brooklyn. Lincoln had never given a major oration in the East before. But he immediately saw the invitation as a huge opportunity to turn himself into a presidential contender. Lincoln quickly agreed to come, as long as he could take a few months to write a proper speech—a "political lecture," he called it. Not until he got to New York did he learn that his appearance had been moved across the river to Manhattan, to Cooper Union, a newly opened college. This change actually worked in Lincoln's favor. Now he would speak in the place where America's most important newspapers had their headquarters. He would speak to a large audience of hundreds, but the newspapers were likely to carry his words to hundreds of *thousands*.

Of course, he decided to focus his remarks on only one topic:

slavery. Senator Douglas had recently written a magazine article insisting America's founding fathers believed that only individual states could choose to welcome or outlaw slavery—not the federal government. The article outraged Lincoln, but it also inspired him. For weeks he worked on a speech that would show just the opposite: that "our fathers," as he called the founders, clearly believed from the first that the federal government had the right to halt the spread of slavery. In fact, as Lincoln learned from studying old books and documents, most of those who had signed the Constitution had later voted against, or spoken out against, slavery. When Lincoln was done arranging these facts into a speech, he had written 7,500 words on dozens of pages of notepaper. Lincoln used no machine to write—none yet existed! He did all his work painstakingly by hand, dipping a pen into an inkwell as he proceeded. He had no secretary or assistant to help him. Busy with his work as a lawyer by day, he spent countless nights laboring on his Cooper Union address.

As it turned out, Lincoln faced a major risk by having asked to delay his trip. Around the time of the invitation from the Young Republicans of New York, an antislavery leader named John Brown, already known for using violent means to overthrow slavery in Kansas, led a band of armed black and white men into Virginia to start what they hoped would grow into a slave revolution. With no warning, they captured and occupied a federal armory at Harpers Ferry, Virginia. Brown was convinced that once enslaved people in the area heard about their arrival, they would quickly run away to join the uprising. John Brown's raid was in one sense a bloody failure. U.S. Marines under future Civil War general Robert E. Lee quickly stormed and recaptured the armory, killed several of John Brown's men, and wounded and captured Brown himself. He was quickly put on trial for treason, found guilty, and hanged in December. But in the words of a tribute song that quickly gained in popularity across the North:

> John Brown's body lies a-mouldering in the grave,
> John Brown's body lies a-mouldering in the grave,
> John Brown's body lies a-mouldering in the grave,
> His soul is marching on!
> Glory, glory hallelujah! Glory, glory hallelujah!
> Glory, glory hallelujah! His soul is marching on.

John Brown either inspired or infuriated Americans of his time. Some believed him a liberator, but others branded him a terrorist. One thing was clear: his raid struck fear into Southern slave-owner society. Now they were convinced that all antislavery men—Lincoln included—meant to use force to confiscate "their property." Even to many Northerners, Brown was considered a madman. But the most liberal whites, the abolitionists, called him a hero, and compared him to Jesus and Moses for sacrificing his life for the freedom of others. Lincoln's challenge in New York was to make sure moderate and conservative Republicans did not think he supported violence of the John Brown type. But he also needed to remind liberal Republicans that he, too, believed in eventual freedom. Striking the right balance would be a very difficult feat. Before leaving for the East, Lincoln tried out his arguments before an audience in Kansas, declaring that he did not object when "old John Brown" was executed. But he acknowledged that Brown died for a just cause because he "agreed with us in thinking slavery wrong."

In late February, Lincoln commenced his long and exhausting journey halfway across the country from Springfield to New York. One pro-Douglas newspaper in Springfield teased him by writing that he was surely heading for a "disappointment." The three-day trip took him over fourteen hundred miles of railroad track. He had to change lines often. None of the trains he rode offered sleeper cars to rest, or dining cars to eat. Mary packed him a picnic basket to take with him, and knitted him a woolen hat to wear when the passenger cars got too cold. Few people would have recognized the man already famous for wearing tall stovepipe hats—he must have looked strange indeed with a woolen cap pulled over his thick black hair.

The long ride was bumpy, uncomfortable, and painfully slow. He arrived in New York City weary, but in good spirits. While there he stayed at a fine hotel, attended church in Brooklyn, and toured the squalid Manhattan slum known as the Five Points. There, he visited a home for poor Irish orphans and encouraged its boys to work hard so they could succeed just as he had.

On the evening of February 27, Lincoln made his way to Cooper Union for the most important speech of his entire career. The "pick and flower" of New York sat in the audience, women as well as men. Around fifteen hundred people paid twenty-five cents each to hear the man from Illinois speak in the college's Great Hall. Many expected the Westerner to be crude and clumsy. In fact, most in the crowd were so shocked by Lincoln's strange appearance, high-pitched voice, and twangy Indiana accent that it was hard at first for them to understand what he was saying. But within a few minutes, they looked past the speaker's homely face, uncombed hair, long arms, and gigantic feet. They began instead paying rapt attention to his clear arguments and compelling ideas. And they quickly fell under his powerful spell. Lincoln all but hypnotized the audience that night. His speech was a triumph. At its end, listeners jumped to their feet and threw their hats in the air.

Lincoln's message at Cooper Union was simple and appealing. Slavery could continue to exist where it already existed. It would eventually die out on its own. But Americans must not let it spread into new territories. If it did, newly elected proslavery senators and representatives would head to Washington in such great numbers that the so-called "slave power" would not only survive but also expand. Southerners, he insisted, had nothing to fear from Republicans. If they would only listen to Republican ideas, they would understand that the party did not threaten their way of life. Still, he affirmed his personal belief that slavery itself was morally wrong. And he all but promised that in time it would cease to exist. "Let us have faith," he assured the crowd, "that right makes might, and in that faith, let us, to the end, dare to do our duty as we understand it."

The next morning, just as Lincoln hoped, four New York newspapers printed his Cooper Union speech word for word, and within weeks, the oration had reappeared in papers across the North. Republicans lavished it with praise and hailed Lincoln as an important new spokesman for the antislavery movement nationwide. Publishers quickly reissued the Cooper Union speech as a pamphlet, and it enjoyed even wider circulation. The speech made Lincoln an overnight success in the media capital of the nation and propelled him to his greatest national fame yet. Suddenly, Republicans throughout the North began speaking of him as a possible candidate for vice president—or even the highest office in the land. The country had found a brave new voice in the fight against the spread of slavery.

While in New York, Lincoln did something else to improve his popularity with the public. He had provided the necessary words; now he would provide the accompanying image as well. Only hours before he was due to speak at Cooper Union, he visited the Broadway studio of the famous photographer Mathew Brady, and there posed for a portrait. Lincoln had sat for photographs before, back in Illinois, but the resulting close-ups usually made him look frighteningly ugly and ill-kempt. The Brady picture came out quite differently. The New York photographer made the Westerner look tall, strong, dignified, and self-confident by posing him alongside a pile of thick books that symbolized wisdom and before a large pillar that suggested leadership.

Even with all these props, Brady was still not quite satisfied with the composition he had arranged, admitting: "I had great trouble in making a natural picture. When I got him before the camera I asked him if I might not arrange his collar, and with that he began to pull it up."

"Ah," said Lincoln to Brady, "I see you want to shorten my neck."

"That's it exactly," came Brady's reply, and as the photogra-

The prominent New York photographer Mathew Brady took this famous photograph of Lincoln on February 27, 1860. Only hours later, Lincoln delivered his career-changing Cooper Union address. He later said the speech and photo "made me president." (Courtesy Library of Congress)

pher later recalled, "the two men laughed." The result, however, was no laughing matter. With Lincoln's scrawny totem of
a neck cleverly hidden, and his giant physique emphasized over
his homely face, Brady's picture was a work of art—and a huge
commercial and political success. A few weeks later, when an
admirer wrote to Lincoln asking for his latest photograph, Lincoln joked: "I think you can easily get one at New-York. While I
was there I was taken to one of the places where they get up such
things, and I suppose they got my shaddow and can multiply
copies indefinitely."

Indeed they could. At the time Brady created the portrait,
photography was just coming into its own. For the first time,
photographs could be reproduced in great quantities and not
only exchanged among friends and families, but also sold in
public. The so-called "Cooper Union" photo inspired prints,
campaign buttons, even cartoons. Lincoln later admitted of his
visit to New York, "Brady and the Cooper Union speech made
me President."

So did the speeches Lincoln made in the days that followed
throughout New England, fulfilling invitations that quickly
came his way after his success in the big city. For the most part
he used those occasions to repeat many of the thoughts he had
expressed first at Cooper Union.

Perhaps the most enjoyable part of Lincoln's trip came when
he reached Exeter, New Hampshire, where his son Robert was
enrolled at prep school. Robert had failed the entrance exams
for Harvard College a few months earlier, and his parents sent
him off to Exeter to take additional courses so he could take the
test again. We do not know whether Robert really wanted to be

schooled in the East, but his father seemed determined to give his son the kind of elite education he had never had an opportunity to pursue himself.

Like all teenagers, Robert was a bit embarrassed when his father came to town and met his school friends. When the elder Lincoln first appeared and sat down on the stage at the Exeter town hall on March 3, Robert's friend Marshall Snow took note of how awkward he looked "all hunched up" and teased: "Isn't it too bad Bob's father is so homely? Don't you feel sorry for him?" But when Lincoln "untangled" his long legs, rose up on the platform and began to speak, as Snow remembered, "his uncouth appearance was absolutely forgotten by us boys. . . . His face lighted up and the man was changed; it seemed absolutely like another person speaking to us. . . . There was absolutely no more pity for Bob; we were proud of his father."

Tired out by his long speaking tour, Lincoln wrote home to Mary the next morning: "I have been unable to escape this toil. If I had foreseen it, I think I would not have come East at all." But surely Lincoln also realized that exactly one year later to the day—on March 4, 1861—a new president would be inaugurated in Washington. After giving eleven widely praised speeches in two weeks, Lincoln for the first time had reason to believe that the man taking the oath of office a year in the future might be himself. He did not dare to say so, even to his wife, but no doubt the exciting possibility was much on his mind as he headed back to Illinois. He was now truly a national figure.

That May, just two and a half months after Lincoln returned home, Republicans from across the country gathered at a convention in Chicago to choose their candidate for the presidential campaign. First they passed a party platform that restated the party's strict opposition to the spread of slavery. Then the delegates got down to the business of choosing a candidate. Despite Lincoln's enormous success in New York, few experts really believed he had a strong chance to win the nomination. Much more famous and politically experienced men wanted the job, and were heavily favored. William H. Seward of New York, the front-runner, had been both a governor and a U.S. senator. But many Western delegates thought he would not appeal to voters in their region. Edward Bates of Missouri was distinguished enough, but many thought him too conservative and too old. Salmon Chase of Ohio boasted a good antislavery record and had also served in high office, but was considered too radical by some, too unlikable by others.

Over the past few years, Lincoln had made the fewest enemies of all of them. The fact that he was a Westerner made him especially appealing. It was believed he could win votes in the safely Republican Northeast, where he had just made such a strong first impression. And he could also compete against Democrats in Western swing states like Indiana and Illinois, without which the party could not hope to elect its candidate to the presidency. Moreover, Lincoln's position on slavery seemed best-suited to win the widest support: he was against its spread, but against its immediate abolition, too. He was liberal enough, but not too radical.

Predictably, Seward led on the first round of balloting, but when he failed to win a majority on the second, his candidacy collapsed. After one more calling of the roll, Republicans abandoned their original favorites, rallied behind the Illinois railsplitter, and nominated Abraham Lincoln for president. Lincoln got the exciting news in Springfield, where church bells rang, crowds poured into the streets, and bands played through the night. Meanwhile, the opposition Democrats had split into two separate parties. Northern Democrats chose Lincoln's old rival Stephen A. Douglas as their candidate for president. But Southerners would not accept him. Douglas's Kansas–Nebraska bill proposed that settlers in each of the new Western territories could put the issue of slavery to a vote, for or against. But the most conservative Southerners agreed with the Supreme Court's Dred Scott ruling, which declared slavery to be legal everywhere in America. Southern Democrats stormed out of the convention, held one of their own, and nominated their own candidate for president, the proslavery Vice President John C. Breckinridge of Kentucky. The political landscape grew more crowded still when another presidential candidate emerged: a Tennessee politician named John Bell, nominated by a new group calling itself the Constitutional Union Party. With the Democratic Party hopelessly split in two, and a fourth candidate in the race, Lincoln enjoyed a huge advantage.

Lincoln did no campaigning that summer or fall. In that era, presidential candidates were expected to say and do nothing at all during this time. Their supporters, even newspaper editors, took to the stump on their behalf. Lincoln respected this tradition, and believed he had already said all he needed to say on the issue of slavery. By then, the Lincoln–Douglas debates had appeared in book form and become a bestseller. Reprints of his Cooper Union speech remained extremely popular, too. Lincoln spent the campaign merely posing for painters and photographers and greeting visitors to Springfield. On the other hand

A button made for the 1860 presidential campaign. It featured an image of Lincoln on one side (as seen above) and on the other, a photo of Republican vice presidential candidate Hannibal Hamlin of Maine. (Courtesy Library of Congress)

Douglas, who was desperate for support, campaigned openly and was greeted with outrage and ridicule. And his appearances did nothing to help him.

On Election Day, Lincoln won only 39 percent of the popular vote nationwide. But he carried the entire North save for New Jersey—more than enough states to bring him a decisive victory in the all-important electoral vote count. Still, no president had ever won such a geographically lopsided victory. Lincoln failed to win a single state in the South. In some slave states, in fact, he polled only a tiny 1 or 2 percent of the vote. In one county in southern Maryland, the other three candidates together won around 1,100 votes. Lincoln received just one. In states in the Deep South, Lincoln's name did not even appear on the ballot.

Charging that this "sectional" victory meant Lincoln could not possibly govern the whole country—and what was more, that he posed a serious threat to the future of slavery—South Carolina seceded from the Union in December, the first state to do so. The Union of states in which Lincoln believed so deeply was crumbling even before he had a chance to lead it.

Between his November 1860 election and his March 1861 inauguration, Lincoln said nothing that might further alarm the South. He did not want to provoke additional states into leaving the Union. But he also refused to reassure Southerners that he meant no harm to them. To do so, he believed, was not only unnecessary, but also unbecoming. It would make him appear almost to be begging for the right to be sworn in as president, which he believed he had earned. And worse, it might give Southerners the idea that he would agree to the spread of slavery in exchange for keeping the country united.

As the first Republican ever elected president, Lincoln also believed he had the power and the right to name thousands of fellow Republicans to government jobs throughout the nation. In those days, presidents appointed not only high officials, but also Indian agents, postmasters, and people in other small jobs. Many of these well-paying jobs were rewards for political support. But since so few Southerners had voted Republican, they now feared that Northern Republicans would be sent to their towns and cities to replace neighbors who had served in government positions for years.

Lincoln tried to assure Southerners that he would move slowly on making appointments, but it was an offer that few in the region were willing to accept. Slavery remained the big issue dividing them, and there Lincoln refused to budge. In a private note to Alexander H. Stephens, a Georgia congressman who had once served side by side with him in the House of Representatives, Lincoln tried one last time to narrow the difference separating North and South. "You think slavery is right, and ought to be extended," he insisted, "while we think it wrong and ought to be restricted—that I suppose is the rub."

The "rub" proved too serious to heal. Lincoln's strong belief in his right to move into the White House, and his refusal to say anything new to please slaveholders, convinced six more Southern states to secede from the Union in January and February 1861: Mississippi, Florida, Alabama, Georgia, Louisiana, and Texas. By the time Lincoln began packing his belongings for the trip to Washington, D.C., these seven states had formed a government of their own. They named the new country the Confederate States of America, and chose Jefferson Davis, a proslavery former senator from Mississippi, to serve as president. Alexander Stephens, the congressman whom Lincoln had privately asked to resist secession, became vice president. The new Confederate constitution made no secret of where this "country" stood on slavery. It openly declared slavery to be not only permanent, but also morally correct. As Lincoln prepared to leave Springfield for Washington there were, in a sense, two American nations, two American presidents, and two theories of what the future should be.

Lincoln departed from his hometown on February 11, 1861, a day before his fifty-second birthday. His son Robert joined the group of bodyguards and reporters on the train that steamed out of town early that morning. Mary and their two younger boys, Willie and Tad, planned to join them the following day. A soft drizzle misted the air as Lincoln boarded his handsomely decorated train. When he appeared at the rear of the caboose to say farewell, Lincoln turned to the hundreds of neighbors gathered at the station under their black umbrellas, and in the most emotional speech he had ever delivered, attempted to sum up both his past life in Springfield and his future challenges in Washington:

My friends—No one, not in my situation, can appreciate my feeling of sadness at this parting. To this place, and the kindness of these people, I owe every thing. Here I have lived a quarter of a century, and have passed from a young to an old man. Here my children have been born, and one is buried. I now leave, not knowing when, or whether ever, I may return, with a task before me greater than that which rested upon Washington. Without the assistance of that Divine Being, who ever attended him, I cannot succeed. With that assistance I cannot fail. Trusting in Him, who can go with me, and remain with you and be every where for good, let us confidently hope that all will yet be well. To His care commending you, as I hope in your prayers you will commend me, I bid you an affectionate farewell.

The Lincolns' journey from Springfield to Washington took eleven days, with many stops in between. All along the route, crowds gathered at railroad stations and hotels and begged Lincoln to speak. But he never approached the personal anguish or reverent faith he had revealed in Springfield. The man who had refused to speak at all during his campaign for president now delivered more than a hundred speeches during his trip to *become* president, although most were short and humorous. He wanted citizens to wait to hear his inaugural address before they decided whether to support secession or fight against it.

At one gathering in Indiana he sounded determined to keep the country together: "By what principle of original right is it that one-fiftieth or one-nineteenth of a great nation, by calling themselves a State, have the right to break up and ruin that nation?" He was clearly worried. But as he lightheartedly told another crowd a few days later in Steubenville, Ohio, "If anything goes wrong, however, and you find you have made a mistake, elect a better man the next time. There are plenty of them."

For the moment, however, only one had been elected to lead. And he was on his way to Washington, determined to do so.

CHAPTER SIX

THE MYSTIC CHORDS OF MEMORY

For the most part, the Lincoln family greatly enjoyed their journey to Washington, D.C. Sixteen-year-old Robert may have had the best time of all. He sang songs all along the train ride as his father's friend Ward Lamon strummed his banjo. From time to time, Bob also drank too much wine and paid too much attention to pretty girls. In Indianapolis, he somehow lost track of the only existing copy of the inaugural address, which his father had given to him to safeguard. Infuriated, Lincoln gave Bob a public tongue-lashing and then leapt over the hotel check-in counter and tore through dozens of grip-sacks before finally finding it. The so-called "Prince of Rails" shrugged off the incident. As he put it, "The old man might as well scold about that as something else." The two were never as close as the president had become to his younger boys, William Wallace (known as Willie) and Thomas (nicknamed Tad).

Willie and Tad certainly created much mischief of their own along the way. They made faces at startled passersby from

The Lincolns' first-born son, Robert Todd Lincoln, as he looked as a young law student at Harvard. (Courtesy Library of Congress)

train windows and scampered around each new town as their mother struggled vainly to keep the excited boys under control. Mary was the guest of honor at dozens of ladies' receptions and proudly joined her husband in carriage processions and at special dinners. While in Columbus, Ohio, Lincoln received word of his official election as president of the United States. The electoral votes had finally been counted in Washington—amidst real fears that Southerners would try to disrupt the process. Army General Winfield Scott had even transported cannon to Capitol

Brady   New York.

The mischievous Lincoln boys who lived in the White House: William
Wallace (Willie), left, and Thomas (Tad), at right, with their cousin
Lockwood Todd. Willie died in 1862 at age eleven. (Courtesy Library of
Congress)

Hill to remind Southerners he would use force to see that the vote-counting went on as scheduled. It did.

So did Lincoln's trip. Wherever he went in what he called his "meandering journey," crowds gathered to see and hear him. Through Indiana and Ohio he traveled, then after a brief stop in Pennsylvania, headed to western New York State. In the tiny village of Westfield, New York, the Lincoln train stopped briefly to take on fuel and water, giving Lincoln the chance to call to the crowd for a little girl named Grace Bedell. The eleven-year-old had written a letter to Lincoln during the campaign suggesting that he grow a beard. Grace thought his face looked entirely "too thin" and believed she could get her father and brothers to vote for him if he would just grow whiskers to make himself better looking. Lincoln had written a now-famous reply saying it would be "silly" to grow a beard so late in life, but shortly after winning the election, he began doing so anyway. Now he wore the thick whiskers for which he became famous. Perhaps he thought it might prove too difficult to shave every day during his train journey to Washington. Or maybe he took Grace's advice after all. In Westfield, he picked her up in his arms in front of the local crowd, planted several "hearty kisses" on her face, and thanked her for her inspiration. Grace was so embarrassed by the attention that she ran away and could not be found until the Lincoln train had long gone. But she felt better soon enough and spent the rest of what proved to be a very long life telling the story of how it was she who suggested that Abraham Lincoln grow a beard.

But not everything about the inaugural journey proved heartwarming. In New York City, where Lincoln had spoken

After an eleven-year-old admirer wrote Lincoln to urge him to grow whiskers to improve his appearance, the president-elect followed her advice—and later thanked her in person on his way to Washington for his inauguration. Here is how Lincoln looked just before his departure, with his new beard sprouting. (Courtesy Library of Congress)

so brilliantly at Cooper Union just one year earlier, crowds now seemed hostile—probably because, for the first time, they included Democrats. What was worse, the Democrat who served as mayor let it be known that he thought New York should secede, too, and set up a kind of independent city. Mayor Fernando Wood's goal was to continue shipping goods in and out of the slave states even if war broke out and interrupted trade between North and South. New York was the nation's largest port, and boats often brought loads of cotton there. It did not seem to bother Wood—or many other New Yorkers—that the cotton had been planted and picked by enslaved people. The sad fact was that New York and other Northern cities had long profited from slave labor in this way. They were extremely reluctant to lose Southern business. Lincoln soon put a stop to talk of New York secession. He simply drawled that he did not believe the nation's "front door" could "set up housekeeping on its own."

Lincoln's inaugural trip was scheduled to take him through just one slaveholding city before he reached Washington: Baltimore, Maryland. The day before he was scheduled to appear there, however, the president-elect learned that proslavery terrorists planned to murder him when he changed trains to board the line heading south to the capital on the final leg of his long journey. His alarmed friends quickly convinced him to cancel his appearance and make new arrangements to sneak through town in the dead of night. With reluctance, Lincoln agreed to the secret plan, and even wore a small hat and shawl on the journey so people would be less likely to recognize him. Lincoln passed safely through Baltimore, but suffered much ridicule for doing so. Opponents branded him a coward. One newspaper scoffed that America's next president had "crept into Washington like a thief in the night." It took days before Lincoln convinced people in Washington that he was serious and ready for business.

Lincoln faced another crisis before taking the oath of office as president. For weeks, a group of older leaders from a number of states, South as well as North, had been meeting at Washington's Willard Hotel to find a way to get the seven Confederate states to abandon secession and return to the Union. They called their meeting the Peace Convention, and the delegates made no secret of their belief that almost any compromise would be acceptable as long as it prevented separation and violence. One of their proposals was to allow slavery to expand all the way to the Pacific Ocean, as long as it did so only in southwestern areas like Arizona and southern California. Of course, Lincoln hated this idea—anything that allowed slavery to spread he had long vowed to fight.

The Peace Convention presented a real test for the little-known president-elect. The delegates were more experienced than he was and thought they knew better how to reverse secession and save the Union. To meet this latest challenge to his authority, Lincoln booked a suite for himself at the same hotel, invited all the delegates to his rooms, and greeted them personally. Many were amazed that he recognized so many of them or knew their names. He impressed all of them, even some of the Southerners, with his dignity and strength of purpose. This was not the "boor" or "clown" they had heard about. He was courteous and kindly, but whenever a Southern delegate ventured a rude comment, he responded strongly "with a ring to his voice and a flash from his eyes." And he certainly made it clear that he would not welcome a plan that allowed slavery to widen its evil presence in the country.

The Peace Convention failed, but Lincoln knew that Congress, too, hoped to enact a compromise before he could take office as president. He sent specific instructions to Senator Lyman Trumbull of Illinois that he would not welcome this effort. "Stand firm," he ordered Trumbull. "The tug has to come, & better now, than any time hereafter." To another member of Congress he urged similar courage: "Hold fast, as with a chain of steel." But just hours before his inauguration, Congress actually passed a Thirteenth Amendment to the Constitution—but not the Thirteenth Amendment that stands today. This one instead promised the very opposite: that slavery would be allowed to survive in the South forever, without any further challenge.

Lincoln did nothing to stop the original Thirteenth Amendment from passing because he believed it had no chance of being ratified by three-fourths of the states and becoming the law of the land. Ironically, one of his first duties as president became the unpleasant task of sending this initial Thirteenth Amendment to all of the nation's governors for their due consideration. It must have pained him to do so. But for a new president in a time of crisis, it was critically important to perform all the duties the law required, however distasteful. Lincoln was right: the amendment was never ratified.

Lincoln's last task before taking office was to finalize his presidential cabinet, no mean feat considering the large egos he wanted to bring into his administration. Lincoln hoped to balance his cabinet with Northerners and Southerners, ex-Whigs and ex-Democrats (for the Republicans were a new party composed of former members of the other two). Typical of presidents of his time, he also wanted to reward the big states that voted for him, particularly New York, Pennsylvania, and Ohio. (Some even whispered that Lincoln's convention managers had promised delegates from those states cabinet appointments for their favorite sons in return for switching to Lincoln.) The problems in creating such a "team of rivals," as historian Doris Kearns Goodwin has called it, became evident as soon as Lincoln began doling out the plum jobs. He convinced Missouri's Edward Bates and Maryland's Montgomery Blair to serve, but decided he could trust no other politician from the South—they might quit the cabinet should their states secede.

Then there were the personal issues dividing these aspirants. New York's William Seward refused to serve in the cabinet if Ohio's Salmon Chase joined, too; Chase would not join the cabinet if Seward did. And neither man would agree to be part of the administration if Lincoln offered a job to Simon Cameron of Pennsylvania, whom many politicians suspected of being corrupt. Remarkably, Lincoln convinced every one of them to enter his cabinet, personal and political differences notwithstanding. Seward became secretary of state, Chase secretary of the treasury, Cameron secretary of war, Blair postmaster general, Bates attorney general, and Caleb B. Smith of Indiana secretary of the interior. When friends in Illinois complained that Lincoln had failed to include a secretary from his own home state, he merely drawled that Illinois needed no representation, because Illinois had the president.

On March 4, 1861, Lincoln rose before sunup and dressed himself in a new black suit he had purchased in Chicago. He rehearsed his inaugural address one more time by reading it aloud to his son Robert, and then walked downstairs, climbed into outgoing President James Buchanan's horse-drawn carriage, and joined a parade down Pennsylvania Avenue from the Willard Hotel to the U.S. Capitol. In one sense, the huge procession must have filled spectators with confidence. "Thousands of Lincolnites lined the streets to cheer," one newspaper reported. Beautifully decorated floats rolled by, and thousands of veterans from former wars marched proudly behind them, waving. But onlookers could also see how many guards rode close to Lincoln's carriage to protect him from potential danger, and how many sharpshooters stood on nearby rooftops, rifles raised, ready to fire at anyone who caused a disturbance. "It seemed more like escorting a prisoner to his doom than a president to his inaugural," one observer lamented.

Lincoln arrived at the Capitol to find five thousand people gathered in the plaza outside to hear him deliver his much-anticipated address. From where he stood he could see the site of the old boardinghouse where he and Mary had lived when he had served in Congress years before, to such little notice. Now, as the nation's new president, he would reveal to all the American people what he intended to do about secession. Would he let the South leave the Union without a fight? Or was he prepared to use force to compel them to return? Lincoln unfolded his thick manuscript, put on his reading glasses, and began reading the speech that everyone had been waiting for. An onlooker remembered, "I never listened to a speaker whose enunciation was so clear and distinct. . . . You not only heard every word that he uttered, but every sentence was most clearly expressed. I believe

The scene at Lincoln's presidential inauguration, March 4, 1861, shows a huge crowd gathered in front of the U.S. Capitol. Lincoln is somewhere under the wooden canopy in the center. (Courtesy Library of Congress)

his voice was perfectly audible to every one of the people who occupied the acres before and around him."

The words themselves were powerful. "Physically speaking," he insisted that day, "we can not separate." Secession would not be tolerated. The Union must remain intact. Lincoln was willing to make some concessions after all. He promised to enforce the much-hated Fugitive Slave Act, infuriating abolitionists.

And he repeated his vow that he would not interfere with slavery where it already existed. But above all, he pleaded with the South to reconsider its rush to leave the Union.

Lincoln left no doubt that he planned to use all his powers as president to enforce the law and reunite the states. He would insist that the mail continue to be delivered in the South. He would require that all federal forts and arsenals in Southern territory remain the property of the U.S. government. And he made it clear that it was up to the South to choose between conflict and peace. As he declared in words clearly directed at unhappy Southerners: "In *your* hands, my dissatisfied countrymen, and not in *mine*, is the momentous issue of civil war. . . . You have no oath registered in Heaven to destroy the government, while I shall have the most solemn one to 'preserve, protect, and defend it.'"

Lincoln had originally planned to end his speech with the harsh question: "Shall it be peace, or a sword?" Instead, he decided to conclude with a more soothing message. He reminded Southerners that they were part of the same country—the product of the same history—as Northerners. North and South, he insisted, had far more in common than they had in dispute. As the thousands on hand listened intently, Lincoln spoke these final, majestic words:

We are not enemies, but friends. We must not be enemies. Though passion may have strained, it must not break our bonds of affection. The mystic chords of memory, stretching from every battle-field, and patriot grave, to every living heart and hearthstone, all over this broad land, will yet swell the chorus of the Union, when again touched, as surely they will be, by the better angels of our nature.

And then a frail, elderly man clad in a long black robe struggled to his feet, Bible in hand, and approached Abraham Lincoln on the Capitol porch. The chief justice of the United States was ready to swear Lincoln in as president. And this was no ordinary chief justice: it was none other than Roger B. Taney, author of the Dred Scott decision, which just four years earlier had declared that people of color had no rights. Now the Constitution required that he officially make a man who believed exactly the opposite the president of the United States. Some of the people on the scene remembered that Taney trembled nervously that day, obviously agitated. But the chief justice dutifully offered the Bible to his longtime political enemy, and Lincoln placed his massive left hand on the cover, raised his right hand, and swore to uphold the Constitution. All of Washington seemed to exhale. Lincoln was president—without incident or harm.

Not everyone cheered the new chief executive's eagerly anticipated inaugural message. Upset by Lincoln's pledge to keep control of federal forts in the South, a Richmond newspaper predicted that "civil war will be inaugurated forthwith." On the other hand the abolitionist *New York Independent* hailed the speech as "the wisest state-paper issued to the American people since the Declaration of Independence." But not all antislavery men were pleased. An outraged Frederick Douglass seemed to hear only the unwelcome news that Lincoln planned to enforce the hated Fugitive Slave Act, and that he recognized Southerners' rights to continue owning slaves without interference from the government. Douglass denounced these pledges as signs of "weakness" and "conciliation towards the tyrants and traitors." In a furious editorial for his newspaper *Douglass' Monthly*, he compared the new president to a "slave hound" and rebuked him as the "most dangerous advocate of slave-hunting and slave-catching in the land."

Much as Lincoln hoped otherwise, the "better angels" of American nature would not prevail. The very afternoon of his inauguration, when Lincoln sat down for the first time at his new desk in the White House, he found an urgent message from a U.S. fort located at the mouth of Charleston harbor in hostile South Carolina. Federal soldiers still held the garrison, but its commander warned that they were fast running out of food and ammunition. If the new president did not quickly send supplies and weapons, the soldiers would have no choice but to abandon their post and allow Southerners to seize it. The place was called Fort Sumter. If Lincoln simply allowed the federal soldiers to leave Charleston, the crisis might pass. Or he might be seen as weak. On the other hand, if he sent supplies, his act could provoke a shooting war. It was in many ways the most important decision of his presidency: peace or a sword?

Most of Lincoln's cabinet advisors cautioned him not to make a stand at Fort Sumter. It was too hard, they argued, to both rearm and defend. But the president proved unwilling to meekly give so valuable a property away to the Confederacy. He hit upon a clever plan. He would not send guns or bullets to Sumter, only food and medicine. He would resupply, but not rearm, it. And he would announce the plan in advance so the South could not regard the effort as an act of hostility by an enemy.

Lincoln's solution was brilliant. If the Confederates allowed the supplies to reach the fort, Sumter would remain in U.S. hands. If they objected and attacked, then the Southerners would bear the responsibility for starting a civil war. As one writer later put it, Lincoln believed it was a case of "heads he wins, tails they lose."

In early April, the president duly announced that he intended to resupply Fort Sumter, and in response, on April 12, 1861, Confederate cannon opened fire. For the next thirty-four hours, thousands of shells poured in on the tiny garrison. Several areas caught fire, and smoke shrouded the installation. It was almost a miracle that no lives were lost—the only casualty was a horse. But Sumter's men had no way to withstand the battering, much less return fire to the shoreline. Finally, on April 13, federal

The event that began the Civil War—the bombardment of Fort Sumter in Charleston, South Carolina—as seen in a Currier & Ives print. (Courtesy Library of Congress)

forces surrendered. The next day, the last of the U.S. garrison left on a ship bound for the North. Lincoln immediately called for seventy-five thousand volunteers to put down what he could only regard as an open rebellion. And he ordered a blockade of all Southern ports.

For more than ten years, Americans had feared that North and South would one day erupt in bloodshed. Now the time had come. The American Civil War—the bloodiest war in the country's history—was underway. And few at the time doubted why the fight began. Some people still insist to this day that the war was all about state's rights. But this is hardly true. The war was caused by secession. And secession was caused by slavery. One issue alone ignited the rebellion: the question of whether the nation could indeed endure half slave and half free.

CHAPTER SEVEN

A PEOPLE'S CONFLICT

Some Americans, especially Northerners, initially believed that the war would be a short one, and for a time, Lincoln hoped that no other Southern states would secede and join the Confederacy. But once he called for troops to fight the rebellion, Virginia, Arkansas, North Carolina, and Tennessee all seceded as well. Only through force and persuasion did the slaveholding states of Missouri, Kentucky, and Maryland remain loyal to the United States. Significant areas of Missouri and Kentucky ended up fighting for the Confederacy anyway. Lincoln forcibly prevented the Maryland state legislature from meeting to consider secession. That was the only way the president could keep that crucial state in the Union, too. A few weeks later, a pro-Confederate mob attacked a trainload of Massachusetts soldiers on their way to Washington as they rode between railroad stations in Baltimore. They were traveling along the very same route that Lincoln himself had refused to follow in daylight just a few weeks before. The attack on the federal troops convinced him he had been right.

Instead of apologizing for the attack, the mayor of Baltimore traveled to the White House to urge the president to find another route for future regiments. A furious Lincoln exploded at him: "You express great horror of bloodshed, and yet would not lay a straw in the way of those who are organizing in Virginia and elsewhere to capture this city. The rebels attack Fort Sumter, and your citizens attack troops sent to the defense of the Government. . . . I must have troops to defend this Capital. Geographically it lies surrounded by the soil of Maryland; and mathematically the necessity exists that they should come over her territory. Our men are not moles, and can't dig under the earth; they are not birds, and can't fly through the air. There is no way but to march across, and that they must do."

Lincoln's tough actions in Maryland aroused much criticism. By suspending habeas corpus—the constitutional protection that guaranteed all prisoners would have their day in court—the government managed to lock away people he considered to be dangerous traitors. By agreeing to let the army shut down several Maryland newspapers, he quieted criticism against the Union. But many Northerners thought this was too high a price to pay for keeping the country whole. Lincoln, they said, was behaving like a tyrant in the name of preserving democracy.

Congress was then in recess, but Lincoln called the House and Senate back into special session on July 4 to defend his actions. In a brilliantly worded message he argued that "this issue embraces more than the fate of these United States. It presents to the whole family of man, the question, whether a constitutional republic, or a democracy—a government of the people, by the same people—can, or cannot, maintain its territorial integrity, against its own domestic foes. It presents the question, whether discontented individuals, too few in numbers to control admin- istration, according to organic law, in any case, can always, upon the pretences made in this case, or on any other pretences, or ar- bitrarily, without any pretence, break up their Government, and thus practically put an end to free government upon the earth." Lincoln's answer was: they could not. Yes, he had suspended the writ of habeas corpus, but as he argued: "are all the laws, *but one*, to go unexecuted, and the government itself go to pieces, lest that one be violated?"

Lincoln made no secret of his belief that the rebels had vio- lated the law first by inventing the idea that any state had "sacred supremacy" over the whole country. He strongly denied that the Constitution gave any state the power to withdraw from the Union without the consent of the Union itself. He never men- tioned slavery directly as a cause of the rebellion, or promised freedom would come as a result. It was still too early.

"This is essentially a People's contest," Lincoln declared in the most famous passage of his message. "On the side of the Union, it is a struggle for maintaining in the world, that form, and substance of government, whose leading object is, to elevate the condition of men—to lift artificial weights from all shoul- ders—to clear the paths of laudable pursuit for all—to afford all, an unfettered start, and a fair chance, in the race of life." And then he added:

Our popular government has often been called an experi- ment. Two points in it, our people have already settled—

the successful *establishing*, and the successful *administering* of it. One still remains—its successful *maintenance* against a formidable internal attempt to overthrow it. It is now for them to demonstrate to the world, that those who can fairly carry an election, can also suppress a rebellion—that ballots are the rightful, and peaceful, successors of bullets; and that when ballots have fairly, and constitutionally, decided, there can be no successful appeal, except to ballots themselves, at succeeding elections. Such will be a great lesson of peace, teaching men that what they cannot take by an election, neither can they take it by a war—teaching all, the folly of being the beginners of a war.

No one, Lincoln included, was very surprised when his ringing message fell on deaf ears in the South. Still, most Northerners believed that the Union Army would quickly crush the upstart Confederates when the two sides finally confronted each other. That occurred in July 1861, when Northern and Southern forces met in battle near the town of Manassas, Virginia, not far from Washington, D.C. Hundreds of Washington's leading citizens packed picnic baskets and headed down to the battlefield to watch the action firsthand, confident that the Union would quickly whip the Confederacy and end the rebellion in a single day. They thought of the event as entertainment. Indeed, Union forces did well at the beginning of the battle. But then the tide turned. Confederate forces counterattacked, and Union troops buckled, fleeing the field so quickly that many of them trampled over the picnic blankets of the terrified spectators. The Battle of Manassas—or Bull Run, as it came to be known in the North—

proved a humiliating disaster for Lincoln and the Union. The war could be a long one after all.

For a time, however, Lincoln continued to believe the North could win the struggle and restore the Union as it was without requiring action against slavery. However, the administration did not discourage slaves from running away once they heard about the fighting, especially if they fled into Union Army encampments and sought work there as laborers. When the first enslaved people did so, a Union general named Benjamin F. Butler decided to let them stay. A Massachusetts Democrat who had supported Southerner John C. Breckinridge for president in 1860—his first choice had been Jefferson Davis!—Butler was the unlikeliest of all antislavery liberators. But confronted with the first arrivals of escaping slaves to Fortress Monroe at Hampton Roads, Virginia, he memorably declared they were "contraband of war." From then on, African Americans escaping slavery on their own became known as "contrabands."

These extraordinarily brave people struck the first real blows against slavery. They also added critical manpower to the Union Army and, by taking on the tasks of manual labor, freed additional white soldiers for actual fighting. Lincoln never directly urged slaves to flee from their owners, but he encouraged contrabands anyway by saying nothing to *discourage* them, and by doing nothing to send them back into bondage. Nevertheless, despite all its advantages, for a time the Union Army won few major victories. The Confederacy seemed to get stronger, not weaker, over time.

The constant tension made life in the White House extremely difficult for the Lincoln family. Mary may have dreamed for

Mary Lincoln—she never used her maiden name "Todd" after her marriage—as she looked as First Lady in a photograph by the Mathew Brady gallery in Washington. (Courtesy Library of Congress)

years of becoming mistress of the president's mansion, but when she arrived in Washington, the town was in no mood for lavish parties or hostesses with grand ideas of themselves. Frustrated, she turned to shopping for clothes she did not need and redecorating the run-down home, even though Lincoln complained that it was "better than any house *they* had ever lived in." When Congress earmarked twenty thousand dollars for the project, Mary spent even more. Her expensive tastes and bad financial judgment in a time of war caused a scandal. When the president learned about it, he was furious. He swore it would "stink in the nostrils" of the American public to buy "flub dubs for that damned old house" while "freezing soldiers could not have blankets." Lincoln offered to pay the extra costs of the White House redecoration himself, but in the end Congress quietly made up the difference.

In February 1862, the Lincoln family suffered a crippling loss when Willie, by some accounts his parents' favorite child, took sick from drinking tainted water at the White House and died of typhoid fever at the age of 11. The loss of Willie sent the president into a deep mourning from which he struggled to emerge so he could continue to lead the nation. Mary, on the other hand, never completely recovered from her son's death. Her sobs filled the White House for months and she continued to wear black for a year. She even consulted psychics who promised to help her communicate with Willie's spirit in the afterworld. To support her, Lincoln reportedly even attended a séance in the White House.

The president had little time to feel sorry for himself. Although for a while he locked himself in his room on the day of the week Willie died, he worked his way out of his own depression and got back to work. In addition to reading and writing several letters every day, he regularly saw military advisers, political associates, and others. Always interested in science and technology, he encouraged inventors to devise new weapons to help beat the rebels, and could occasionally be seen on the lawns near the White House firing experimental rifles. He approved construction of the first ironclad warship, a decision that helped the Union win the naval war. Lincoln also spent a few hours, twice a week, seeing strangers who lined up outside his door—

"as if waiting to be shaved in a barber's shop," Lincoln joked—to ask for favors, pardons, and other personal help. When a worried friend asked him to cancel these sessions because of the strain on him, Lincoln refused. Tired as he was, he felt he must continue to see the people who elected him. "They don't want much, and they don't get but little," he explained, "and I must see them." He called his weekly open houses his "public opinion baths," and defended them by explaining, "It would never do for a president to have guards with drawn sabers at his door, as if he fancied he were . . . an emperor."

War news, meanwhile, offered little reason for good cheer. Except for a few victories in the West under the command of a rising general named Ulysses S. Grant, the Union continued to struggle to restore national authority in the South. As Union generals were discovering, whatever their advantages in men and weapons, it was difficult to fight a war in Southern territory, where Confederate soldiers were far more familiar with the terrain and had a keen passion to, as they saw it, protect their homeland from invaders. The fact was that after a year of fighting, the Union was still divided and many weary Northerners appeared willing to give up the fight and let the South go its separate way in peace.

Lincoln disagreed. In the spring of 1862, he began searching for a new way to reverse the Union's bad luck. And he came to the conclusion that the only way to shorten the war, save lives, and reunite the states was to strike a blow against slavery. If he could begin at last to rid the country of the horrendous condition that had triggered secession and war in the first place, better still.

From the beginning of the contest, Lincoln believed the war gave him unheard-of power to crush the rebellion almost any way he chose. His administration shut down newspapers that differed with him, and threw critics of the war into jail without trials. Many Northerners objected. Yet in his first year and a half as president, Lincoln still hoped to end the Civil War without really touching slavery in a major way.

The reasons for his reluctance were extremely complicated. First, he felt he had little power to act in places that did not even recognize him as president, especially once the Union Army began losing battles. Such was surely the case in the eleven states of the Confederacy. But Lincoln had also convinced several slaveholding states to remain in the Union. Slavery was still legal in Maryland, Delaware, Missouri, and Kentucky. But none had seceded—so far. The president worried that if he ordered slaves freed anywhere in the nation, these Border States would abandon the Union, too. Worse, Union soldiers might literally throw down their rifles, desert, or simply return home, unwilling to fight a war to free black people. If Maryland quit the Union, then Washington D.C., which sat within its borders, could no longer remain as the national capital. The government itself might have to flee. If Kentucky left, the whole West might be lost to the Confederacy forever. "I would like to have God on my side," Lincoln is said to have joked at the time. "But I *must* have Kentucky."

For a while, Lincoln sent mixed signals to the country where slavery was concerned. When two of his army generals, John C. Frémont and David Hunter, issued unauthorized orders of their own freeing slaves in the areas they commanded, Lincoln promptly overruled them. He insisted that only he had the right to act against slavery. The abolitionist community hurled much criticism at the president for these decisions. But when Congress passed bills giving courts the right to take away Confederates' slaves as a punishment for rebellion against the government, Lincoln signed the measures into law. As he well knew, however, no Southern court was ever likely to issue such a ruling.

In April 1862 Lincoln approved another law—one that at last outlawed slavery in Washington, D.C. Lincoln had been hoping to ban slavery in the capital ever since he first served there in Congress in the late 1840s. The bill was not perfect—it offered generous compensation for slave owners and imposed a kind of apprentice labor system on younger African Americans. But it did mark the first time in the history of the United States that the government had ever officially moved against slavery. African Americans and white abolitionists celebrated the milestone enthusiastically.

To keep the antislavery momentum going, the president next invited congressmen from the loyal slave states to visit him at the White House. He proposed to them that the U.S. government buy slaves from their owners and gradually set them free. It was cheaper, he reminded them, for the country to pay for slaves than to pay for a long and costly war. The slaveholders themselves would lose no money. And the pressure on the South to end the rebellion would increase. But the border-state congressmen ultimately turned down the humane and generous offer. Disappointed, Lincoln finally concluded that he must use his powers as president to do what the generals could not, and the courts and Congress would not. Throughout that spring, however, Union armies suffered so many additional setbacks that Lincoln felt he could not yet act. Moreover, his slow-moving commanding general, George B. McClellan, told Lincoln that he would never support a war to free slaves—and warned that his soldiers would not, either. If Lincoln acted, he hinted, the army would "rapidly disintegrate."

Frustrated by a general who would neither fight nor consider emancipation as another weapon to win the war, Lincoln

THE FIRST READING OF THE EMANCIPATION PROCLAMATION BEFORE THE CABINET

Lincoln reads his earliest draft of an Emancipation Proclamation to his cabinet on July 22, 1862. Artist Francis B. Carpenter created this scene as an oil painting two years later, from which A. H. Ritchie fashioned this hugely popular print. Ironically, at the meeting it portrays, Lincoln's cabinet convinced the president not to issue his proclamation just yet. (Courtesy Library of Congress)

dismissed McClellan. On July 22, 1862, he summoned his cabinet for a crucial meeting at the White House. Most of these men had opposed slavery as long and as sincerely as he had. When they were seated around the table in Lincoln's office, the president excitedly told them his dramatic news. He was now prepared to free slaves in the Confederate states. He read aloud to them a brief document he had prepared for publication. It was not yet finished in his usual brilliant style. Still, it is possible that July 22 might have become the nation's emancipation day. Instead, to the president's surprise, most members of the cabinet expressed the belief that emancipation was a bad idea. The war had been going so badly, one of them pointed out, that Americans might regard such an announcement as an act of desperation—"a last shriek, on the retreat." Lincoln was disheartened but he heeded their advice. He issued no proclamation that day. As his advisers suggested, he would wait until the North finally won a major battle.

CHAPTER EIGHT

FAIR WARNING ON SLAVERY

The desperately needed Union victory did not come quickly. In fact, later that summer Lincoln's forces lost the next major battle they fought against the Confederates. The latest catastrophe occurred at the Second Battle of Bull Run. "Oh, what a terrible slaughter," the "heart sick" president told a visitor. "Those dreadful days! Shall I ever forget them? No, never, never."

Lincoln had no choice but to return George McClellan to command. Convinced that military success must surely come eventually, the president continued to work away at a more polished version of his emancipation order. He decided it would take the form of a warning, giving rebels until a specifically chosen date to throw down their arms, affirm their allegiance to the government, or risk losing their valuable slave property. But the president continued to fret that no matter how he couched emancipation—no matter how carefully he worded it, and no matter how much notice he gave Southerners before it took effect—he would suffer a huge political setback whenever it was issued.

No one of the day understood public relations better than Abraham Lincoln. In the days before broadcast news and political polling, he seemed to sense exactly how far he could go on any issue. Given the choice between acting aggressively and moving slowly, Lincoln almost always chose to be cautious. Where slavery was concerned, he feared that making emancipation sound like a first step toward black equality would instantly lose him the support not only of the Border States, but of the vast majority of white people in the North—and not just Democrats. Racism was widespread in 1860s America, North as well as South, and with the fall 1862 congressional elections fast approaching, dissatisfaction with Lincoln on the issue of race would almost certainly lead to major political setbacks for Republicans.

To limit such consequences, Lincoln not only kept his emancipation plans secret for a time, he made a number of statements designed to convince people he would strike a blow against slavery only if it would help save the Union, and not because it might help people of color. Worse, at least to modern eyes, he made it clear to white and black people alike that he still believed free African Americans should leave the country and begin new lives in Africa or the Caribbean. Looked at from the twenty-first century, these statements make Lincoln look almost racist himself. But in 1862, they echoed mainstream white American thought. And Lincoln sincerely believed he must utter them or risk another revolution, this time within the North, which would have doomed emancipation anyway.

But in his efforts to prepare the country for freedom, the president may have gone too far. On August 14 he summoned a delegation of free African Americans to the White House to discuss colonization. On one hand, the event marked an important first for equality: no group of black people had ever been welcomed to the executive mansion for any reason. But once they were assembled, Lincoln read a statement that seemed to suggest that *they*, not Southerners, had caused the war. "Perhaps you have long been free," Lincoln told them, "or all of your lives. Your race are suffering, in my judgment, the greatest wrong inflicted on any people. But even when you cease to be slaves, you are yet far removed from being placed on an equality with the white race. You are cut off from many of the advantages which the other race enjoy. The aspiration of men is to enjoy equality with the best when free, but on this broad continent, not a single man of your race is made the equal of a single man of ours. Go where you are treated the best and the ban is still upon you."

On this occasion, Lincoln seemed to come close to placing blame on African Americans for causing the Civil War. "We look to our condition," he insisted, "owing to the condition of the two races on this continent. I need not recount to you the effects upon white men, growing out of the institution of Slavery. I believe in its general evil effects on the white race. See our present condition—the country engaged in war!—our white men cutting one another's throats, none knowing how far it will extend. . . . I repeat, without the institution of Slavery and the colored race as a basis, the war could not have an existence. It is better for us both, therefore, to be separated."

The delegation received this disheartening recommendation with extraordinary grace, agreeing to seriously consider the president's proposal. But African American newspapers promptly denounced both the scheme and the president. For one, Frederick Douglass harshly condemned Lincoln for using "the language and arguments of an itinerant Colonization lecturer, showing all his inconsistencies, his pride of race and blood, his contempt for Negroes, and his canting hypocrisy." He called Lincoln "a genuine representative of American prejudice and Negro hatred." Of course, Douglass and Lincoln's other critics had no idea at the time that the president had already decided to issue an emancipation proclamation and was deliberately waiting for the right time to announce it.

In fact, a good case can be made that Lincoln called the meeting with free blacks specifically to pave the way for emancipation. By reminding whites that he still favored attempts to resettle blacks, he limited the potential risk from an emancipation order he had already written and was merely waiting to reveal.

The president's next opportunity to express cautionary thoughts about emancipation occurred in August, when *New York Tribune* editor Horace Greeley bitterly condemned the Lincoln administration for being "strangely and disastrously remiss" for not working harder or faster to free slaves. The editor demanded that Lincoln do what "Loyal Millions of your countrymen require of you." The president wrote a reply, widely published in newspapers throughout the North, insisting that while he might yet act just as Greeley suggested, he would do so only if it helped end the war and restore federal authority in the South. He wrote:

My paramount object in this struggle *is* to save the Union, and is *not* either to save or destroy slavery. If I could save the Union without freeing *any* slave I would do it, and if I could save it by freeing *all* the slaves I would do it; and if I could save it by freeing some and leaving others alone I would also do that. What I do about slavery, and the colored race, I do because I believe it helps to save the Union; and what I forbear, I forbear because I do *not* believe it would help to save the Union. I shall do *less* whenever I shall believe what I am doing hurts the cause, and I shall do *more* whenever I shall believe doing more will help the cause.

The only hint of what Lincoln really intended to do came in the final words of this famous letter. Only then did he point out that his statement represented only his view of "*official* duty." As he concluded, on a far more hopeful note, "I intend no modification of my oft-expressed *personal* wish that all men every where could be free."

By then word slowly began leaking out that Lincoln indeed had a draft proclamation waiting for announcement whenever the Union Army enjoyed a battlefield success. Lincoln no doubt managed these leaks himself, too, hoping to head off more criticism from antislavery men like Greeley. It was a political balancing act of exquisite delicacy.

By the end of summer, with no military successes in sight, Lincoln was clearly becoming exasperated by his inability to act on slavery. When yet another delegation visited the White House on September 13—this time composed of antislavery ministers from Chicago—Lincoln burst out: "What *good* would a proclamation of emancipation from me do, especially as we are now situated? I do not want to issue a document that the whole world will see must necessarily be inoperative, like the Pope's Bull against the comet! Would *my word* free the slaves, when I cannot even enforce the Constitution in the rebel States?"

But then Lincoln abruptly changed his tone. As he assured his startled visitors: "Do not misunderstand me, because I have mentioned these objections. They indicate the difficulties that have thus far prevented my action in some such way as you desire. I have not decided against a proclamation of liberty to the slaves, but hold the matter under advisement. And I can assure you that the subject is on my mind, by day and night, more than any other." Lincoln ended this strange monologue by leaving the matter to a higher power: "Whatever shall appear to be God's will I will do." By this time, Lincoln was waiting not only for a signal from God, but also one from General McClellan. For he had just learned that the Army of Northern Virginia had invaded Maryland and was heading for a confrontation with the Union's Army of the Potomac.

The long-awaited, desperately needed Union victory finally occurred on September 17, at the Battle of Antietam, near the town of Sharpsburg, Maryland. The bloodiest day in the history of American warfare, it proved less than a perfect triumph. More than 4,700 died at Antietam, and more than 18,000 lay wounded. Worse, Union commander George B. McClellan allowed General Robert E. Lee and his rebel troops to escape back to Virginia, disappointing Lincoln. But the win was enough for the president to make his move. He had made a pact with God that if the Union won, he would issue the proclamation.

Lincoln confers with General George B. McClellan in a tent at army headquarters near Antietam in October 1862. Lincoln wanted McClellan to attack Confederate forces again. When McClellan hesitated, the president fired him. Alexander Gardner took this picture—the first photograph of an American president on a battlefield of war. (Courtesy Library of Congress)

Five days later, on September 22, Lincoln summoned his cabinet back to the White House for the long-awaited follow-up meeting on emancipation. To break the tension, he began the meeting by reading aloud from a humorous book, which irritated some of the grimmer officials. Then Lincoln's voice took on a "graver" tone and he slowly announced: "Gentlemen: I have, as you are aware, thought a great deal about the relation of this war to Slavery; and you all remember that, several weeks ago, I read to you an Order I had prepared on this subject which, on account of objections made by some of you, was not issued. Ever since then, my mind has been much occupied with this subject, and I have thought all along that the time for acting on it might very probably come. I think the time has come now."

This time, Lincoln did not want to hear his cabinet officers' opinions on the main issue, which he customarily welcomed. "When the rebel army was at Frederick," he explained, "I determined, as soon as it should be driven out of Maryland, to issue a Proclamation of Emancipation such as I thought most likely to be useful. I said nothing to any one; but I made the promise to myself, and—to my Maker. The rebel army is now driven out, and I am going to fulfill that promise."

That very day, Lincoln issued his "Preliminary Emancipation Proclamation," a warning that stated the South had a hundred days to give up the rebellion or he would issue a final emancipation order freeing their slaves forever. He made no speech that day to explain his actions; he merely sent his handwritten manuscript to be inscribed as an official government document and had copies sent to the newspapers for publication. The text appeared the following morning for all people to read. Citing his powers as "Commander-in-chief of the Army and Navy of the United States," Lincoln made absolutely clear that if the rebellion did not end on January 1, "all persons held as slaves" in the confederacy would be "then, thenceforward, and forever free." The government, Lincoln further pledged, would not only "recognize and maintain the freedom of such persons," it would encourage "any of them, in any efforts they may make for their actual freedom."

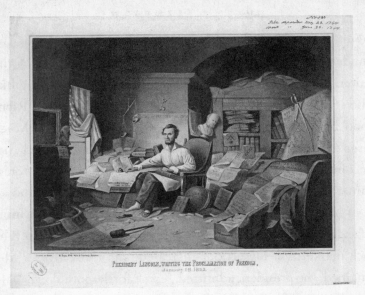

Artists showed how Lincoln was inspired to write the Emancipation Proclamation in different ways—depending on whether they approved of it or not. Artist David Gilmour Blythe depicted Lincoln holding the Bible and the Constitution to inspire him. (Courtesy Library of Congress)

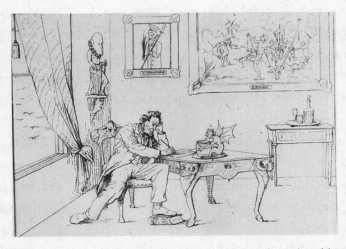

Pro-Confederate etcher Adalbert Volck, on the other hand, showed Lincoln rudely resting his foot on the Bible, and drawing his ink—and we are meant to believe, his inspiration— from Satan. (Courtesy Library of Congress)

Not everyone cheered. Many Democrats warned that the thunderbolt proclamation would divide what was left of the Union. Some complained bitterly that Lincoln was acting like a dictator. One newspaper in the Confederate capital of Richmond branded him a "coward, assassin, [and] savage." Much closer to home, the pro-Democratic *Chicago Times* charged that Lincoln had "cut loose from the constitution. . . . We protest against it as a monstrous usurpation, a criminal wrong, and an act of national suicide." What was worse, as the president himself sadly admitted, many Union soldiers reacted badly, too. The stock market fell. Desertions increased, and those troops who remained, the president admitted, "come forth more slowly." He worried that he would lose the country's support. Privately, he admitted, "I hope for greater gain than loss; but of this I was not entirely confident." To a crowd of supporters who gathered outside the White House on September 24 he sounded only slightly more hopeful. To cries of "Bless you" and "No Mistake," the president declared: "What I did, I did after very full deliberation, and under a heavy and solemn sense of responsibility. I can only trust in God I have made no mistake. It is now for the country and the world to pass judgment on it, and, may be, take action upon it."

Some critics passed judgment by bemoaning the proclamation's ungraceful prose. But the respected antislavery writer Ralph Waldo Emerson called the proclamation a "dazzling success," adding: "one midsummer day seems to repair the damage of a year of war." New York editor Theodore Tilton, one of the local Republicans who had welcomed Lincoln to Cooper Union just three years before, felt much the same way. He sent the president a brief but grateful telegram: "*God bless you* for *a good deed!*" And the proclamation thrilled Frederick Douglass, dry style notwithstanding. "We shout for joy," he exulted, "that we live to record this righteous decree. *Abraham Lincoln*, president of the United States, Commander-in-Chief of the army and navy, in his own peculiar, circuitous, forbearing, and hesitating way, slow but one hopes sure, has, while the loyal heart was near breaking with despair," proclaimed freedom. "Free forever! oh! long enslaved millions, whose cries have so vexed the air and sky, suffer on a few more days in sorrow, the hour of your deliverance draws nigh!"

But the president felt no such sense of deliverance. Rather, the hundred-day deadline tested Abraham Lincoln's nerve, and in a sense put the North itself on trial. Would it accept this truly revolutionary challenge and begin fighting for freedom as well as the Union? Or would white people refuse to do battle for black people? For three months, the debate raged and Lincoln worried about his own future, and that of the nation. The people themselves spoke for the first time in the fall elections. To the president's disappointment, voters harshly punished the Republicans at the polls. Lincoln's party lost representatives in Congress, and in state legislatures, too. New York elected a Democratic governor, as did several other Northern states. It was not unusual for a sitting president's party to lose seats in Congress during an off-year election. But Lincoln had hoped for far better. After all, most Southern voters did not even go to the polls in the fall of 1862. This rejection had come only from the Northern and Border States. And it stung Lincoln hard. Fearing that the entire North would rise up against his administration, Lincoln fired

General McClellan a second time on November 5 and named Ambrose E. Burnside the new commander of the Army of the Potomac.

Under Burnside, however, things went from bad to worse. In mid-December, the Union Army suffered one of its most staggering defeats yet at the Battle of Fredericksburg. Some twelve thousand soldiers fell in a single, unsuccessful attack against Lee's Confederates. In the days to come, Burnside's retreating army bogged down in winter mud. To his despair, the president then learned that Burnside's fellow generals had begun to criticize him openly for his failures. While all this was happening, a group of Republican senators tried to force the president to fire some of his cabinet officers and reorganize the entire government.

"We are on the brink of destruction," a desperate Lincoln told a friend. "It appears to me the Almighty is against us and I can hardly see a ray of hope." Whether the Emancipation Proclamation would take effect on January 1 as scheduled was anyone's guess.

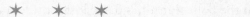

CHAPTER NINE

THE DAY OF JUBILEE

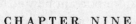

In spite of all the bad news from both voters and battlefields, New Year's Day 1863 found Washington, D.C., in the mood for a celebration.

For one thing, the president of the United States was bravely hosting a holiday reception at the White House. The public was invited to attend. Cabinet officers would be on hand. Military officers were scheduled to attend in their splendid uniforms.

True, the bloody Civil War had been raging for nearly two years and showed no signs of ending soon. Hundreds of thousands of soldiers had already died of wounds or disease. Tens of thousands more were badly wounded, many crippled for life. Millions on both sides mourned the loss of husbands, fathers, sons, and brothers. But the American Union still survived. The flag still waved over the nation's capital. A new year was beginning. Perhaps it would bring both peace and healing to the divided United States. But most of all, this new year was destined to bring forth something truly historic. For the first time, most Americans understood that if Lincoln indeed issued the final

Emancipation Proclamation that day, then 1863 would launch the country toward an important new goal: freedom.

As guests prepared to flock to the White House to celebrate the holiday with their president, Abraham Lincoln faced the most important decision of his life: would he, in the end, do what no American leader had ever tried to do before? Would he summon the moral and political courage to strike a death blow against two hundred years of slavery—the horrific system that kept nearly three million human beings of African descent in captivity and made them nothing more than property in the eyes of the law?

"He will stand by the Proclamation!" predicted the *Chicago Tribune*. "We have never doubted Abraham Lincoln. . . . Least of all, have we ever had any doubt of the firmness of his anti-slavery convictions." But a worried New York lawyer named George Templeton Strong wondered whether "Lincoln's backbone" would "carry him through the work he is pledged to do." As Strong put it: "If he come out fair and square, he will do the biggest thing an Illinois jury lawyer has ever had a chance of doing, and take high place among the men who have controlled the destinies of nations. If he postpone or dilute his action, his name will be a byword and a hissing till the annals of the nineteenth century are forgotten."

Like Lincoln, George Templeton Strong was a Republican. Most Democrats, even in the Northern States, believed Lincoln lacked the authority to free slaves by presidential order. Congress had not authorized him to do so. And the Constitution still protected slavery itself. Some newspapers predicted that if Lincoln acted to free slaves, more soldiers would desert and the economy might collapse. Even the president's own wife, Mary, reportedly advised the president to let the emancipation deadline pass.

But Abraham Lincoln had made up his mind. He had waited a long time—too long, some of his liberal critics had complained—to issue the preliminary proclamation the previous September. As Lincoln had recently assured a delegation of Union men from his native Kentucky, he "would rather die than take back a word of the Proclamation of Freedom." And as he informed an Indiana congressman: "The South had fair warning, that if they did not return to their duty, it should strike at this pillar of their strength. The promise must now be kept, and I shall never recall a word."

Exactly one month earlier, on December 1, Lincoln had sent the House and Senate his Annual Message to Congress, to be read aloud by a clerk, as was the custom of the day. This was an important speech—the equivalent of today's State of the Union address. In it, he left little doubt that he planned to go through with the Emancipation Proclamation as committed. "The dogmas of the quiet past," he wrote, "are inadequate to the stormy present. The occasion is piled high with difficulty, and we must rise with the occasion. As our case is new, so we must think anew, and act anew." Then he ended the eloquent message with these especially stirring words:

Fellow-citizens, *we* cannot escape history. We of this Congress and this administration will be remembered in spite of ourselves. . . . No personal significance, or insignificance, can spare one or another of us. The fiery trial through which we pass, will light us down, in honor or dishonor, to the latest generation. We *say* we are for the Union. The world will not forget that we say this. We know how to save the Union. The world knows we do know how to save it. We—even *we here*—hold the power, and bear the responsibility. In *giving* freedom to the *slave*, we *assure* freedom to the *free*—honorable alike in what we give, and what we preserve. We shall nobly save, or meanly lose, the last best, hope of earth. Other means may succeed; this could not fail. The way is plain, peaceful, generous, just—a way which, if followed, the world will forever applaud, and God must forever bless.

Now history was knocking on the White House door. It was New Year's Day. The hour had come.

That morning, a clerk brought Abraham Lincoln the finished document to sign. A professional penmanship expert had prepared it. The words were beautifully inscribed on heavy, parchment-like paper. It began with the line "By the President of the United States of America: A Proclamation." At the bottom of the scroll was the gold seal of the nation, adorned with colorful ribbons. Abraham Lincoln put on his spectacles, picked up the document, and began reading it carefully. He trusted his own writing perfectly, but he wanted to make sure it had been copied without a mistake.

All seemed fine until he got to the final paragraph. It was supposed to say: "In witness whereof, I have hereunto set my hand and caused the seal of the United States of America to be affixed." But something was wrong. The words were garbled. The sentence made no sense. The same words had appeared correctly on dozens of presidential proclamations of much less importance. Yet somehow they were incorrect on the most dramatic announcement of his presidency. So Lincoln decided not to sign it. It was simply too important to make it official with such a flaw. Instead, he instructed that it be sent back to the official scribe who had labored so hard to create it. Holiday or not, he was to start from the beginning and rewrite the entire proclamation.

Lincoln then headed downstairs from his second-floor office and joined the holiday party in the big East Room of the White House. Wearing a black suit, white shirt, and large black bow tie, his huge hands squeezed into white gloves, the tall president stood high above the crowd and greeted his guests, one by one. From noon until two p.m., the public joined the famous men and women on the receiving line. For hours, Lincoln remained at the event, mingling with friends, colleagues, and strangers alike. If he was anxious about the task that awaited him upstairs, he did not show it.

Meanwhile, in cities across the North, free African Americans and white liberals known as "abolitionists"—men who long believed slavery should be outlawed—had been gathering in churches since midnight to wait for the glorious news they believed would soon be coming. They sang hymns, prayed together, and offered speeches. They nervously shared their excitement and their hope for the future. But most of all, they waited—and waited some more. The morning ended, the afternoon began, and still no word came across the telegraph wires from Washington to announce that Lincoln had signed the Emancipation. The agonizing delay continued.

Because the words of the proclamation itself were not inspiring, many artists issued editions that showed the document surrounded by scenes contrasting slavery and freedom. (Courtesy Library of Congress)

Finally, in mid-afternoon, Lincoln got word that the rewritten document was ready for him at last. Excusing himself from his last remaining guests, he climbed the stairs and returned to his office. The partygoers were departing now, and the noise and music that had filled the mansion for so many hours was beginning to subside. The president approached the long wooden cabinet table where he often wrote letters and speeches. He sat down in his usual chair at the head of it. A fire probably blazed in the hearth to warm him from the winter cold. Once again, Lincoln spread the document before him and read it through another time. No photographer stood by to take a picture of this great moment. No artist sat near with sketchbook in hand. In fact, only three witnesses had entered the room: Secretary of State William H. Seward, his son Frederick (who also served as his private secretary), and Lincoln's own private secretary, John G. Nicolay. Together, they looked on as the president finished reading.

The proclamation unrolled before them made clear that the Southern states had failed to heed the president's "fair warning." Rebels would thus lose their slaves forever. Most of the document was given over to mentioning small areas where emancipation would *not* be required—or, as Lincoln saw it, legal. These were areas where the Union had already taken firm control of Confederate territory. Technically, they were no longer "in rebellion." Lincoln felt he had no choice but to exempt them from his order. Otherwise, as a "fit and necessary measure for suppressing" the rebellion, Lincoln ordered that slaves in Confederate areas "are, and henceforward shall be free." He urged freed slaves to "abstain from all violence" and "labor faithfully for reasonable wages," but also added that ex-slaves would for the first time be "received into the armed service of the United States."

Artist Edward D. Marchant portrayed Lincoln wearing a formal white tie to sign the final Emancipation Proclamation—and as he writes his name, the chains on a statue entitled "Liberty" symbolically break in the background. This image was painted for Independence Hall in Philadelphia—though it never made it there. (Courtesy Union League of Philadelphia)

The document ended with the words: "And upon this act, sincerely believed to be an act of justice, warranted by the Constitution, upon military necessity, I invoke the considerate judgment of mankind, and the gracious favor of Almighty God." Lincoln finished reading the document one final time. This time around, the president found no errors in his order. The moment to make the order official had finally arrived. Abraham Lincoln picked up one of the steel-tipped pens that sat on his table, dipped it into an ink bottle, and moved his hand to the spot on the document where he was meant to sign. Suddenly, surprisingly, he put the pen down. Then he lifted it up again and went through the same motions, only to place it down once more. The small group of onlookers must have wondered: Had he changed his mind? Would he actually decide *not* to sign the Emancipation Proclamation after all?

Lincoln looked up and explained himself. "I have been shaking hands since 9 o'clock this morning, and my right arm is almost paralyzed. . . . Three hours' hand-shaking is not calculated to improve a man's chirography [an old-fashioned word for handwriting]. . . . If my name ever goes into history it will be for this act, and my whole soul is in it. If my hand trembles when I sign the Proclamation, all who examine the document hereafter will say, 'He hesitated.'" He did not, he said, want his signature to look "tremulous."

So Lincoln resumed his silence and slowly began rubbing his numb, giant hands together, over and over again until the feeling in them returned. Only then did he at last pick up his pen one more time and write out a firm, bold "Abraham Lincoln." Looking up from the scroll he smiled proudly and said, "That will do."

To some, however, the Emancipation Proclamation did not do enough. To be sure, it was revolutionary. It was the first important order against slavery ever issued by an American president. It ordered the Union Army to free slaves wherever it marched in the South. It encouraged black men to join the ranks of the military for the first time. But the proclamation had its limits. Areas of the Confederacy already captured by the Union—including parts of Louisiana near New Orleans—would not have to surrender their slaves. The western counties of Virginia had broken away to form their own state. West Virginia entered the Union on this same day, January 1, 1863. Very few slaves dwelled there, but they too would remain in bondage.

What seemed more disappointing to some was the dry and dusty style Lincoln had again used for his final proclamation. Some immediately hailed it as the "second Declaration of Independence." But the original Declaration began with the words "When in the course of human events." Lincoln's document began with the dull word "Whereas." Every American knew that the president was capable of superb writing. But he had used none of his flair, none of his power to inspire. Instead, he had chosen to craft a document that crossed every *t* and dotted every *i*. Style did not matter. He was not giving a speech; he was issuing an order as the commander in chief in time of war. The result may have proved boring, but Lincoln believed no court could ever prove it was unlawful. These words were not meant to excite anyone. And by and large they did not.

Many antislavery leaders had clearly hoped for something more inspiring from the final proclamation. The great African American leader Frederick Douglass was one of them. Even after campaigning mightily for the document to be issued, he could not hide his disappointment in the final result. Even so, Douglass instantly appreciated the proclamation's impact. "Law and the sword can and will in the end abolish slavery," he predicted. "That this war is to abolish slavery I have no manner of doubt." Antislavery newspapers hailed the proclamation as a historic breakthrough. "[L]et us thank God for Abraham Lincoln," cheered the *Chicago Tribune* in one such tribute. The headline in the abolitionist paper *The Liberator* pronounced: "The Proclamation. Three Millions of Slaves Set Free: Glory, Hallelujah!" But the proclamation elicited severe criticism as well. "Lincoln is made Dictator of all the North," raged a newspaper in Richmond. In England, the *London Times* gave its reluctant blessing to the idea of emancipation, but criticized Lincoln for waging war to "conquer" the South. Democrats in the North protested that Lincoln had fallen under the influence of radical abolitionists. The president ignored all these attacks. This was no longer about politics; it was about justice. Now he was fighting for something more than Union. He was fighting for liberty.

"No human power can subdue this rebellion without using the Emancipation lever as I have done," Lincoln told a visitor. In the president's own words, the Emancipation Proclamation was not only "the central act of my administration," but also "the great event of the nineteenth century."

✳   ✳   ✳

CHAPTER TEN

FIGHTING FOR FREEDOM

I t is not true of course that the Emancipation Proclamation freed all of the nation's four million slaves. But it is also not true that it freed no slaves at all. In fact, thousands went free on the very day Lincoln signed the historic document. A number of enslaved people living in places like the Sea Islands of South Carolina successfully claimed their liberty under its terms on January 1, 1863. Freedom came as well that day to slaves living in pockets occupied by Union troops in Alabama, Virginia, Georgia, and Arkansas. All together, between twenty thousand and fifty thousand slaves went free on New Year's Day. And Secretary of State William Seward later estimated that, eventually, the proclamation freed two hundred thousand enslaved African Americans. Nevertheless, millions more had to wait.

Americans of the day immediately compared the Emancipation Proclamation to the Declaration of Independence. And with good reason. After all, the Declaration of Independence had not freed all Americans on July 4, 1776—the day it was issued—either. Colonial soldiers had to fight on for the liberty that the founding document proclaimed, and it took years of struggle to fulfill its promise. Like the British, the Confederates did not surrender their so-called property at the mere stroke of a pen. Just as in the War of Independence, Lincoln's armed forces in the Civil War now had to fight to liberate Confederate territory under the terms of the proclamation. What the document certainly did accomplish on the day it was issued was to give the army the immediate authority to free slaves at every country plantation and city home they encountered. The Emancipation Proclamation transformed the war to save the Union into a war to destroy slavery. It launched the march to freedom.

To make sure soldiers clearly understood their new obligation toward freedom, Lincoln quickly "armed" his troops with tiny copies of the proclamation. These booklets were easy to ship to army encampments. And they were convenient for individual soldiers to carry with them on their campaigns into the South. Thereafter, if a Southern civilian questioned a Northern regiment's authority to free his slaves, the officer in charge could simply produce his printed proclamation and insist on the right to do so.

The proclamation changed one important relationship virtually overnight: the Lincoln administration's shaky diplomatic ties with England, which for months had hinted it might recognize the Confederacy as an independent country. Once Lincoln issued the Emancipation Proclamation, all talk of English intervention in American affairs quickly evaporated. Although the British prime minister at first criticized the proclamation, English public opinion overwhelmingly favored freedom. Writing from London, where he assisted his father, the U.S. minister to England, young Henry Adams cheered, "The Emancipation Proclamation has done more for us than all our former victories and all our diplomacy." The Emancipation Proclamation effectively kept England out of the Civil War.

The white soldiers actually fighting the war in America, however, did not all react with similar enthusiasm. When its soldiers first heard the news that Lincoln had issued the proclamation, a regiment from the president's own home state of Illinois promptly deserted, swearing to "lie in the woods until moss grew on their backs rather than help free slaves."

The proclamation certainly had an immediate effect on the Union Army—not only on its size, but in a way, its color. On the heels of Lincoln's order, Congress passed the federal Enrollment Act on March 3, 1863. It created the first military draft to provide new manpower for the Union armed forces. Significantly, it made free African Americans eligible for the first time to join up as well. A few days later, Secretary of War Edwin M. Stanton gave the army the official order "to arm, uniform, equip, and receive into the service of the United States" the first "volunteers of African descent." That same month Lincoln's War Department officially opened its first Bureau of Colored Troops. Frederick Douglass issued a proclamation of his own entitled "Men of Color, to Arms!" Three weeks later, Lincoln wrote to Andrew Johnson, the pro-Union military governor of Tennessee, to urge him to recruit black soldiers, too. Johnson was a longtime slaveholder but now Lincoln wanted him to radically change his views and embrace black enlistment. "I am told you have at least *thought* of raising a negro military force," he began. "In my opinion the country now needs no specific thing so much. . . . The colored population is the great *available* and yet *unavailed* of, force for restoration of the Union. The bare sight of fifty thousand armed, and drilled black soldiers on the banks of the Mississippi," he predicted with pride, "would end the rebellion at once."

Lincoln quickly authorized black recruitment in occupied areas of Florida, Louisiana, and the Mississippi Valley as well. Some commanders in the field, however, resisted. Lincoln's military aide Henry Halleck ordered an initially reluctant General Grant to free "all the slaves you can, and to employ those . . . to the best possible advantage against the enemy." General William T. Sherman stubbornly believed "The Negro . . . is not the equal of the white man," while Burnside claimed that the "enrollment of these negroes is what the loyal people fear." Lincoln overruled them both. As he told a group of church leaders visiting the White House in May, he "would gladly receive into the service not ten thousand but ten times ten thousand colored troops." Their help was crucial, he said, because they would provide "essential service in finishing the war." By June 30, 1863, the first regiment of "U.S. Colored Troops" mustered into service at Washington. By war's end, nearly 179,000 black men had served in its ranks, and another 9,600 in the U.S. Navy.

For a time, Lincoln and Stanton worried that white privates, too, would resent the arrival of black regiments and refuse to fight with them, even though the black units would be entirely separate and segregated and commanded only by white officers. To make more certain that white soldiers supported the new arrivals, Lincoln agreed at first to pay black recruits a lower salary than white soldiers earned. Moreover, while white soldiers re-

The Emancipation Proclamation authorized the enlistment of African American troops for the first time. Some 180,000 went on to serve in the armed forces. Here a new member of the so-called U. S. Colored Troops poses proudly with his family, probably just before going off to war to fight for freedom. (Courtesy Library of Congress)

ceived a bonus to help them pay for their uniforms, black soldiers were forced to repay the *government* for their outfits; the cost of the uniforms was deducted from their pay. White privates earned thirteen dollars per month plus three dollars for clothing; black troops received only ten dollars a month, and had three dollars of that deducted for uniforms.

Many troops who had never thought twice about slavery changed their opinions after they saw slaves firsthand once they marched into the South. Nevertheless, many soldiers still insisted that if the war changed direction they would be "sorry" they ever joined up. In one regiment, desertions rose alarmingly after news came of the emancipation, but a sergeant in an Indiana regiment spoke for many of his fellow soldiers when he said, "[I]f there can be negroes enough to conquer the rebels let them do it." Before long soldiers white as well as black were marching to a new war song:

> We will welcome to our numbers the loyal, true and brave
> Shouting the battle cry of freedom!
> And although they may be poor, not a man shall be a slave,
> Shouting the battle cry of freedom!
> The Union forever! Hurrah, boys, hurrah!
> Down with the traitor, up with the star;
> While we rally round the flag, boys, rally once again,
> Shouting the battle cry of freedom!

Although some cynical white officers predicted that black soldiers would flee at the earliest sign of danger, the first African Americans in combat proved them wrong. On June 7, some three thousand Confederates attacked an all-black unit at Milliken's Bend, Louisiana. Though the African American defenders had no previous experience in battle, they rallied and fought back bravely and successfully.

No African American unit ever won more glory in the war than the 54th Massachusetts earned in July of that year on a narrow beach near Charleston, South Carolina, the city where the Civil War had begun more than two years before. The elite all-black regiment had been organized under a young white abolitionist colonel named Robert Gould Shaw. Union commanders planning the attack on Charleston decided that to succeed they needed first to conquer a strong rebel earthwork fortification known as Battery Wagner, which was blocking their way. The 54th volunteered to lead an attack against the fort on the evening of July 18. The brave troops came astonishingly close to breaching its earthen walls, but were unable to seize the redoubt and suffered a staggering number of losses. One observer who saw the pile of bodies littering the area after the attack claimed that "no battlefield in the country has ever presented such an array of mangled bodies in a small compass." Among the pile of dead lying in the heap of casualties before Battery Wagner was Shaw himself and dozens of his gallant black soldiers.

Despite the extra danger black troops faced from angry Southern whites, enthusiasm remained high. "I am a soldier now," one proud African American recruit, Samuel Cabble, wrote to his wife, "and I shall use my utmost endeavor to strike at the rebellion and the heart of this system that so long has kept us in chains."

Lincoln did not react personally to the sacrifices of the 54th Massachusetts. But in appreciation of their valor—and the loyalty of men like Private Cabble—he declared that he would do his utmost to protect black troops from cruelty. Earlier, infuriated over black enlistment in Northern armies, Confederate President Jefferson Davis had warned that captured black soldiers would either be "put to death" or sent into slavery, even if

STORMING FORT WAGNER.

The 54th Massachusetts Regiment—the most famous of all African American units—in their famous, doomed 1863 attack on Battery Wagner in South Carolina, a postwar chromo by Kurz & Allison of Chicago. (Courtesy Library of Congress)

they were free to begin with. Lincoln responded with an unmistakable threat of his own. "The law of nations" and the "customs of war as carried on by civilized powers," he declared, "permit no distinction as to color in the treatment of prisoners of war as public enemies. To sell or enslave any captured person, on account of his color, and for no offence against the laws of war, is a relapse into barbarism and a crime against the civilization of the age." Vowing that the Union Army would "give the same protection to all of its soldiers," black or white, Lincoln ordered that "for every soldier of the United States Army killed in violation of the laws of war, a rebel soldier shall be executed; and for every one enslaved by the enemy or sold into slavery, a rebel soldier shall be placed at hard labor."

Meanwhile, the nagging issue of equal pay would not go away. In August 1863, Frederick Douglass called at the White House to plead with Lincoln to offer equal pay for black troops. Douglass remembered that Lincoln's handshake was "not too warm or too cold." When the president urged him to speak out to recruit even more black volunteers, Douglass insisted that to enlist more African Americans, Lincoln must agree to do four things:

First—You must give colored soldiers the same pay that you give white soldiers. Second—You must compel the Confederate States to treat colored soldiers, when taken prisoners, as prisoners of war. Third—When any colored man or soldier performs brave, meritorious exploits in the field, you must enable me to say to those that I recruit that they will be promoted for such service, precisely as white men are promoted for similar service. Fourth—In case any colored soldiers are murdered in cold blood and taken prisoners, you should retaliate in kind.

Lincoln listened to his "little speech," Douglass remembered, " . . . with earnest attention and with very apparent sympathy." But the president insisted that "prejudice" among whites still made it impossible to treat black soldiers equally for the present. Besides, in Lincoln's view, black soldiers "had larger motives for being soldiers than white men; that they ought to be willing to enter the service upon any conditions." The president did admit that unequal pay was a "terrible remedy" but pledged that it was only temporary. "I assure you, Mr. Douglass," Lincoln concluded, "that in the end they shall have the same pay as white soldiers."Lincoln finally approved equal pay on June 15, 1864.

Lincoln would soon enlist Douglass in the battle for freedom in an entirely different way. When others actually suggested that Lincoln consider returning to slavery the heroic black "warriors" of Port Hudson and the Battle of Olustee, "and thus win the respect of the masters they fought," Lincoln was adamant. "Should I do so," he declared, "I should deserve to be damned in time and eternity."

For a time Lincoln must have thought he was damned indeed. In early June 1863, the Union suffered another terrible defeat at the Battle of Chancellorsville, Virginia. Disheartened, Lincoln named General George G. Meade to head the Army of the Potomac as Lee moved north into Pennsylvania. A few weeks later, federal forces under Meade did win the largest and bloodiest battle yet fought in the war, a three-day confrontation in and around the tiny town of Gettysburg. Publicly, Lincoln praised "the many brave officers and soldiers who have fought in the cause of the Union and liberties of the country." But privately, he was dissatisfied. Meade allowed Robert E. Lee's crippled Confederate Army to escape back South. Lincoln believed Meade might have won the entire war had he pursued and beaten Lee before he could cross the Potomac River into Virginia. The frustrated commander in chief sat down and wrote Meade a long letter, congratulating him for the "magnificent success you

Frederick Douglass—escaped slave, abolitionist, editor, orator, and adviser to Lincoln—the most prominent and influential African American leader of the nineteenth century. (Courtesy Library of Congress)

gave the cause of the country at Gettysburg," but bluntly point-
ing out his disappointment over Meade's failure to pursue Lee
afterward. "He was within your easy grasp," Lincoln continued,
"and to have closed upon him would . . . have ended the war.
As it is, the war will be prolonged indefinitely. . . . Your golden
opportunity is gone, and I am distressed immeasurably because
of it." Typical of his careful leadership style, Lincoln vented all
his anger by composing this tough letter. Then he thought better of it and decided not to send it to Meade after all. Instead
he filed it away, marked "never sent, or signed." By this time, at
least, Lincoln had received more good news from the battlefield,
this time from Mississippi. For months, General Grant had laid
siege to the hilltop city of Vicksburg, bombarding it into sub-
mission. The day after the Confederates surrendered was July 4,
and Lincoln called it the happiest Independence Day since the
founding of the republic.

The Union victory at Gettysburg all but ended the threat
that the Confederacy could or would invade the North again.
The capture of Vicksburg showed the power of the Union Army
in the West. For a time, Lincoln must surely have believed the
war might in fact be coming to a close. He would never have so
guessed, but it was at this point only halfway over.

Personal problems made it almost impossible for Lincoln to
concentrate on his work during this period. For the second
summer in a row, the Lincoln family had moved into a cottage
called the Soldiers' Home north of Washington. Situated on a
hill overlooking the capital, the breezes there made it easier to

tolerate Washington's stifling heat. And it allowed the unhappy Mary Lincoln a place to rest privately, away from the gaze of her critics, some of whom actually thought she was a Southern spy. At the Soldiers' Home, she wrote a friend, "[W]e can be as secluded as we please."

At the time, Mary had few friends left in Washington. Among them was a free African American seamstress named Elizabeth Keckly. Mary often treated her as no more than a servant. Once, she revealed some of her incurable race prejudice when she wrote in what she thought was a flattering recommendation that "although colored," Lizzie was "very industrious." But Mrs. Lincoln became deeply attached to Keckly and the feeling for a time was mutual. Lizzie helped Mary survive the tragedy of Willie's death and introduced her to the suffering of fugitive slaves living in squalor around the capital. Once, Lizzie led Mary on a personal tour of one of the city's crowded contraband camps. There, Mrs. Lincoln was shocked to see people "without bed covering and having to use any bits of carpeting to cover themselves, many dying of want." In response, she donated two hundred dollars to buy supplies for the homeless fugitives. She did not ask her husband for the money; she simply told him to forward the funds.

Around the time of the Battle of Gettysburg, an unknown would-be assassin tried to do Lincoln harm. He loosened one of the wheels of the carriage the president used to commute between the Soldiers' Home and the White House each day. On the day the wheel came off, however, Mary, not her husband, was riding inside. After her frightened driver jumped from the rig, Mary too leaped to the road, where she struck her head on a rock. She seemed at first to recover, but then developed an infection and lingered near death for days. Lincoln sent for his son Robert, due home from Harvard for his annual summer vacation, but Robert delayed his arrival to watch a dramatic event unfolding in New York City in response to the first military draft in the nation's history.

There, angry residents opposed to serving against their will in the Union Army—especially the idea of fighting for black freedom—began setting fires, ransacking homes, and attacking white Republicans and innocent African Americans. Robert apparently thought the street battles something of an adventure, because he lingered on in New York, forcing his worried father to send him an urgent message: "Why do I hear no more of you?" By this time, rioters had set fire to a number of buildings, tore through the homes of local antislavery leaders, dragged black people through the streets, and even burned down the so-called "Colored Orphan's Asylum." Lincoln ordered exhausted troops from Gettysburg to put down the disturbance.

Robert finally arrived back home, where he belatedly helped take over the supervision of his mother's care. But Mary took a long time to heal and seemed more nervous and unpredictable than ever when she did. Robert later said his mother was never the same again after her carriage accident. For her part, Mary admitted she sometimes felt like she was drowning in "*deep waters*" that seemed at times to "overwhelm" her.

But she was well enough to take a summer vacation to New England with Robert and Tad later that July. The mountains seemed to refresh her. While Mary and the children were away, Lincoln missed them enormously. When they had still not returned to the White House by late September, Lincoln wrote her what sounds very much like a love letter. "The air is so clear and cool, and apparently healthy, that I would be glad for you to come," he scribbled. "Nothing very particular, but I would be glad to see you and Tad." When his wife failed to reply, Lincoln dashed off a more direct message the following day: "I really wish to see you."

Mary had always hoped that her husband's election to the presidency would bring them closer together. For the first time in their lives, she believed, they would spend all their time under the same roof. But things did not turn out as she planned. Lincoln spent hours at work, developing closer relationships with politicians, not his wife. Mary lost most of the influence she once felt she had over him. Mary thought she saw him less than when he was a traveling lawyer back in Illinois.

To one friend she admitted, "I consider myself fortunate, if at eleven o'clock, I once more find myself, in my pleasant room & very especially, if my tired & weary Husband, is *there*, resting in the lounge to receive me—to chat over the occurrences of the day."

The Civil War divided many American families, and the Lincolns were no exception.

CHAPTER ELEVEN

UNFINISHED WORK

Frederick Douglass had been among the many critics who regretted the absence of eloquence from Lincoln's Emancipation Proclamation. But soon enough, Lincoln provided the political "poetry" to amplify the dry prose of the proclamation. One of his first opportunities came in August 1863. Lincoln's old Springfield, Illinois, neighbors had invited him back home to speak at a rally in support of the Union war effort. The president very much wanted to go. He had heard that Springfielders did not like his Emancipation Proclamation, and opposed the arming of black troops as well. Here was a golden opportunity to explain his new policies in the place where his political career had begun. In the end, Lincoln was too busy to take the time such a trip would have required. But he wrote a speech for the occasion anyway and asked one of his old Springfield friends to read it "very slowly" to the expected crowd.

The remarks proved breathtaking. Lincoln began by admitting that many of his old friends "dislike the emancipation proclamation." But then he bluntly told them "it can not be retracted, any more than the dead can be brought to life." Black people, he added, "like other people, act upon motives. Why should they do any thing for us, if we will do nothing for them? If they stake their lives for us, they must be promoted by the strongest motive—even the promise of freedom. And the promise being made, must be kept."

And then, for good measure, Lincoln confidently predicted that peace would soon come. "And then," he warned, "there will be some black men who can remember that, with silent tongue, and clenched teeth, and steady eye, and well-poised bayonet, they have helped mankind on to this great consummation; while I fear, there will be some white ones, unable to forget that, with malignant heart, and deceitful speech, they have strove to hinder it."

Here at last was authentic freedom poetry—the "bleeding heart," one contemporary declared, pulsating beneath the "iron." No less a writer than Harriet Beecher Stowe, the author of *Uncle's Tom Cabin*, called Lincoln's powerful Springfield letter the expression of "a mind both strong and generous," and concluded that Lincoln's words were "worthy to be inscribed in letters of gold." It was probably the greatest speech Abraham Lincoln never gave.

Some three months later, Lincoln outdid himself with the greatest speech this president—and probably any president— ever delivered. He returned to the scene of the most famous and furious encounter of the entire Civil War: Gettysburg. There he was invited, almost as an afterthought, to offer "a few appropriate remarks" about the sacrifices that had been made there by Union soldiers. The occasion was the dedication of a new cemetery for the Union men killed in the war's biggest battle.

The president was not the main speaker that day. That honor

Lincoln (center, bare-headed) arrives on the speaker's platform at the Gettysburg National Soldiers' Ceremony on November 19, 1863. Some two hours later, he would deliver his most famous speech: the Gettysburg Address. (Courtesy Library of Congress)

belonged to a famous old orator named Edward Everett, who spoke to the crowd for more than two hours. Then Lincoln rose and spoke for just two minutes. Yet his 270 words carried immense power. He never once mentioned slavery or slaves, emancipation or black troops. But he somehow managed to remind the country and the world that America would ever after be dedicated to equal opportunity for all:

Four score and seven years ago our fathers brought forth on this continent, a new nation, conceived in Liberty, and dedicated to the proposition that all men are created equal.

Now we are engaged in a great civil war, testing whether that nation, or any nation so conceived and so dedicated, can long endure. We are met on a great battle-field of that war. We have come to dedicate a portion of that field, as a final resting place for those who here gave their lives that that nation might live, it is altogether fitting and proper that we should do this.

But in a larger sense, we can not dedicate—we can not consecrate—we can not hallow—this ground. The brave men, living and dead, who struggled here, have consecrated it far above our poor power to add or detract. The world will little note, nor long remember what we say here, but it can never forget what they did here. It is for us the living, rather, to be dedicated here to the unfinished work which they who fought here have thus far so nobly advanced. It is rather for us to be here dedicated to the great task remaining before us—that from these honored dead we take increased devotion to that cause for which they gave the last full measure of devotion—that this nation, under God, shall have a new birth of freedom—and that government of the people, by the people, for the people, shall not perish from the earth.

Lincoln's speech is known today as his masterpiece, but in its own time, not everyone applauded it. Republicans heaped praise on the address, but many Democrats denounced it as an embarrassing failure—"silly, flat, and dishwatery," said one. The politically motivated reaction to Lincoln's most brilliant oration came as no real surprise. The countdown had begun to the next presidential election, and as Lincoln well knew, the results of that crucial contest would decide, once and for all, whether slaves would remain free or return to bondage.

Unimaginable as it may have seemed, a victory by Democrats in 1864 would likely have meant cancellation of the Emancipation Proclamation. In part, Lincoln decided he must win reelection to give the proclamation more time to work. Although no president since Andrew Jackson had won a second term, Lincoln made it clear he would ask the voters to choose him for another four years. He enjoyed drawling that he based his decision on the old expression "It's better not to change horses in midstream." But he also believed that unless he remained in the White House, the Union might die and slavery might live.

Advisers who thought that Lincoln would win only if he stopped the war, recognized the Confederacy, and canceled the Emancipation Proclamation, did not understand the president's determination. "I think I shall not retract or repudiate it," he told one of his generals that year. "Those who have tasted actual freedom I believe can never be slaves, or quasi slaves again."

On his way home from Gettysburg, Lincoln suddenly fell ill. His African American aide, William Johnson, placed a wet cloth on his head for the train ride home. When he got back to the White House, doctors told the president he was suffering from a mild form of smallpox and ordered him to bed. In a way, Lincoln enjoyed his rest. He joked that his secretaries should send everyone looking for a job or a favor to his bedside. "Now," he said,

A photograph of Lincoln by Alexander Gardner, 1863. (Courtesy Library of Congress)

"I have something I can give everyone." During Lincoln's illness, William Johnson took excellent care of the president, but
eventually caught smallpox himself, no doubt from being in such
close contact with someone suffering from the disease. Johnson

was not as fortunate as Lincoln—probably because he did not have a William Johnson to take care of him! A few weeks later, the loyal White House valet died of smallpox himself. Lincoln paid for his tombstone. It bore a simple but eloquent inscription:

WILLIAM JOHNSON

Citizen

The president was still under the weather at Christmastime when he received a gift of sorts that must have lifted his spirits immensely. It came from none other than William de Fleurville, or "William Florville the Barber," as he signed himself. For nearly three years, Lincoln had received not one pleasant letter from his hometown. Most messages from Springfield included demands for assistance or appointments. But William Florville's note was different. He wanted Lincoln to know that he was sorry to have heard about Willie's death, and hoped the president would tell his son Tad that the dog the children had left behind in Springfield was "alive and Kicking." He also wanted Mrs. Lincoln to hear that the tenants who had rented their old home had kept it "in good order."

But most of all he wanted to be sure that Lincoln knew that since emancipation, African Americans considered Lincoln to be a "truly great Man." Thanks to you, Florville wrote, the "Shackels have fallen, and Bondmen have become freemen to Some extent already under your Proclamation. And I hope, ere long, it may be universal in all the Slave States." Florville added that he yearned for the day when "your authority may soon extend over them all, to all the oppressed, relieving them from their Bondage, and cruel Masters; who make them work, and fight, against the Government."

And when the country's troubles finally do end, the president's old friend, barber, and law client confidently predicted, "the Nation will rejoice, the oppressed will Shout the name of their deliverer, and Generations to come, will rise up and call you blessed."

At the end of 1863, however, Lincoln was not so certain he was blessed. In fact, he was not so sure he would even survive the forthcoming election.

CHAPTER TWELVE

YEAR OF DECISION

Lincoln's decision to run for a second term as president seemed courageous to some, outrageous to others. Not for thirty-six years had a sitting president sought reelection to the White House. And no leader anywhere in the world had ever placed his name before the voters in the midst of a civil war.

Some Americans feared—and others hoped—that Lincoln would cancel the election altogether and simply announce he would stay in power as long as the rebellion continued. How after all could a country at war with itself conduct a peaceful presidential election? But Lincoln would have none of it. He considered the election "a necessity." As he explained it, "We can not have free government without elections; and if the rebellion could force us to forego, or postpone a national election, it might fairly claim to have already conquered and ruined us. Win or lose, he would take his case to the people of the Union and ask for a vote of confidence.

But Lincoln's path to victory in 1864 proved rocky. Early in the year, his secretary of the treasury, Salmon P. Chase, tried hard to interest fellow Republicans in the idea of dumping Lincoln and nominating someone else for president—namely, Chase himself. Lincoln exposed the scheme, and Chase was embarrassed enough to resign from the cabinet, his hopes dashed. Disgruntled Republicans turned next to General Ulysses S. Grant. Thinking him far more popular than the president, they pressured him to challenge Lincoln. But Grant refused to be disloyal to his commander in chief.

Later, Lincoln faced yet another challenge from one of his generals: John C. Frémont. Eight years earlier, Frémont had been the very first Republican ever to run for president. He lost that election. And he had achieved little on the battlefield since. As a Union general in the West, however, Frémont had in 1861 tried to free all the slaves within the area he commanded. Lincoln insisted that as commander in chief, only he had the power to emancipate slaves as a military measure. He asked Frémont to revoke his order. When the general balked, Lincoln directly ordered him to cancel his proclamation, and the general had no choice but to obey. The controversy cost Lincoln some early support among liberal Republicans who thought he had been too slow to act against slavery. Now, when Chase dropped out of the race for the Republican nomination, Frémont emerged as an independent, third-party alternative to Lincoln. If four candidates could run for office in 1860, his supporters reasoned, then perhaps three could run in 1864.

By then, of course, the president had issued the Emancipation Proclamation. Yet some antislavery Republicans still considered Frémont a more reliable antislavery man. Besides, even though his military record was undistinguished, the general had once been a greatly admired explorer and, as a millionaire, could afford to finance his own campaign.

More important, the likelihood loomed that a Democratic successor would proclaim that Union soldiers need no longer free enslaved people wherever they encountered them in the Confederacy. To take the slavery issue directly to the president, the Democrats nominated former General George B. McClellan, whose Antietam victory in 1862 had allowed Lincoln to issue the preliminary Emancipation Proclamation in the first place. McClellan himself had fiercely opposed emancipation and had made his feelings known to the president. Now he would run on a "peace" platform calling on North and South to stop fighting—whatever that might mean to enslaved African Americans.

In the end, Lincoln proved too deft a politician for all the enemies in his own party. When a group of liberal Republicans called a convention of their own and nominated Frémont, Lincoln calmly offered to dismiss his loyal postmaster general, Montgomery Blair. A pro-Union Marylander, Blair had been an important ally of Lincoln's throughout the years of the war. But liberals disliked him, believing he did not care enough about emancipation. When Blair left the president's cabinet, the third-party Frémont candidacy collapsed, and Republicans had little choice but to unite around their president. As early as March, two Republican congressmen predicted that Lincoln would defeat Democrats and "slave Kings" alike.

By the time Republicans gathered for their own convention at Baltimore in June, Lincoln had no more opponents from within his own party, and he was renominated. To widen the appeal to voters, the Republicans renamed themselves the National Union Party. But then its leaders made a fateful mistake. The man serving as vice president, Hannibal Hamlin, was an anti-slavery man from Maine. He had seemed the ideal choice for the second spot back in 1860, when Lincoln was a little-known Westerner. Hamlin was a prominent Easterner and provided a perfect balance for the ticket.

By 1864 however, East and West no longer seemed to matter. So the newly named Union Party looked to a Southerner—a Union man from the South who opposed the rebellion—to balance the new slate. It chose the only Southern U.S. senator who had refused to join the Confederacy after his state seceded: Andrew Johnson, now serving as military governor of Tennessee. Johnson did believe passionately in the Union. Though he hailed from a slave state and was no friend of the African American, he had also come to accept the fact that slavery was heading for extinction. It is still not known for sure whether Lincoln himself, or Republican politicians acting on their own at Baltimore, substituted Johnson for Hamlin. In those days, such decisions were usually left to delegates at the convention. Lincoln did not even travel to Baltimore to attend the event himself. But whoever thought Johnson would make a good vice presidential nominee committed a terrible error. Johnson may have provided the desired regional balance to the 1864 ticket, but he lacked Lincoln's humanity and was not in any sense prepared to be president himself. As it turned out, he would later have to take over the job anyway.

Of equal importance, the 1864 Union convention also adopted a party platform setting forth its core beliefs for the

ABRAHAM LINCOLN.   ANDREW JOHNSON.

Lincoln's campaign for reelection in 1864 downplayed the controversial emancipation issue. This typical poster, showing the president and his new vice presidential running mate Andrew Johnson, instead showed ships and symbols of prosperity. (Courtesy Library of Congress) future. Platforms were very serious business in the nineteenth century. And Lincoln very much wanted the new party platform to do something no other declaration of party principles had ever done before: pledge to abolish slavery everywhere.

The only way to achieve full freedom was to amend the U.S. Constitution, an extremely difficult process. First, two-thirds of all U.S. senators and two-thirds of all U.S. representatives would have to vote yes. Then, three-fourths of each of the state legislatures had to approve the amendment. The process could be frustrating and time-consuming. Nonetheless, Lincoln took pains to make his wishes known to the delegates gathered at Baltimore. He wanted freedom to be "utter and complete." And only a constitutional amendment could make his wishes utterly and completely legal. The idea seemed logical enough. The Emancipation Proclamation had declared the government to be opposed to slavery and had successfully begun the process of freeing slaves. But further action was clearly needed in the states that were exempted from the presidential order of January 1, 1863—meaning Border States like Kentucky, Missouri, and Delaware, where slavery remained legal.

Lincoln had other reasons to desire passage of a constitutional amendment. Although his proclamation carefully declared slaves in the Confederacy to be "then and thenceforward" free, Lincoln knew that his order had yet to be reviewed by the Supreme Court. And Roger B. Taney, who had authored the hateful Dred Scott Decision back in 1857, was still serving as chief justice at the incredibly advanced age of eighty-seven. To some it seemed Taney might live forever and, if he got the chance, would surely rule to overturn emancipation. In fact, the ancient justice had already composed the draft of a decision that held Lincoln's proclamation unconstitutional—and a case had not even come before the court!

Meanwhile, the Union Army, fighting in the South, could only occupy so much territory and free so many slaves. By now the armed forces under the overall leadership of General Grant had redirected their strategy. At Lincoln's urging, the army had changed its goal from that of conquering Southern cities to that of destroying Southern armies. This new emphasis was wise, but it meant that soldiers were now less likely than before to find and free large numbers of enslaved people. Clearly, a new and broader policy was urgently required.

That Lincoln's proclamation had gone far—but not far enough—was evident in a sad letter the president received that summer from a slave named Annie Davis.

> Mr president
> It is my desire to be free. to go to see my people on the
> eastern shore. my mistress wont let me you will please
> let me know if we are free. and what I can do. I write
> to you for advice. please send me word this week. or as
> soon as possible and oblidge.

But Annie Davis was *not* free. As an enslaved resident of Bel Air, Maryland, a Union slave state, the Emancipation Proclamation did not apply to her case. Only a constitutional amendment could help enslaved people in Border States like Maryland. But just before Annie Davis wrote her letter, liberals in her home state in fact began a move to end slavery there even before the new Thirteenth Amendment came up for debate. Crucial support came from the Eastern Shore, the slaveholding area where Annie Davis lived. Maryland's U.S. Senator Reverdy Johnson called this development the beginning of "a new era" in his state, and perhaps for the entire country in the eyes of the world.

Still, Lincoln and his fellow Republicans felt a constitutional amendment was required, even though the process for its adoption might be extremely challenging. Then, just as now, Americans considered their Constitution an almost sacred document. After its enactment in 1787, some states had only grudgingly approved the first ten amendments focused on individual liberty, freedom of speech, and freedom of the press—a package of amendments called the Bill of Rights. But since then, only two other amendments had won approval, one clarifying judicial power and the other creating the Electoral College.

The Constitution itself had never mentioned "slavery" by name, though it did refer to persons "held to service as labor." According to the Constitution, a slave counted as three-fifths of a person for purposes of measuring state population. This meant that Southerners enjoyed special advantages in allocating congressmen even though millions of the people they represented had no rights. The provision disgusted freedom-loving Americans. But because it was enshrined in the Constitution, it would be extremely difficult to dislodge. Now, at Lincoln's direction, the 1864 Republican platform called for an "amendment to the Constitution . . . as shall terminate and forever prohibit the existence of slavery within the . . . jurisdiction of the United States."

As summer faded into autumn, Lincoln genuinely came to believe that he would lose the presidency to McClellan come

November. It was then that he again demonstrated his zealous belief in freedom, this time in a way so private that few people knew about the extraordinary gesture. It began when Lincoln summoned Frederick Douglass back to the White House and confided to him his dim prospects for reelection. Lincoln frankly admitted that emancipation was in jeopardy. But he had an idea. Could not Douglass, a master at recruiting soldiers, now enlist a small army of African Americans to head into the Confederacy with a new assignment, not to fight but to alert slaves still held in captivity that they should flee while they still had the chance?

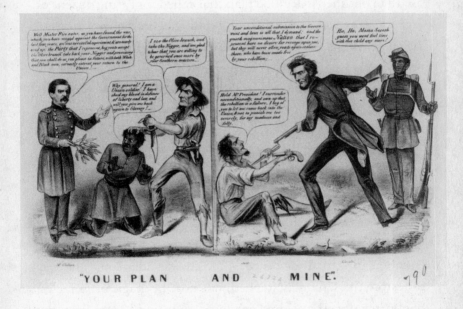

This 1864 pro-Republican political cartoon sharply contrasted Lincoln—placing African Americans in uniform and subduing Confederate President Jefferson Davis—with his opponent, George B. McClellan, making peace with Davis and threatening an ex-slave. (Courtesy Library of Congress)

Lincoln believed that if enslaved people attained freedom while he remained in office, no court would ever send them back into slavery. The challenge was to liberate as many slaves as possible before November, in case he should lose and emancipation die along with his presidency.

Douglass quickly embraced Lincoln's desperate plan for urging slaves "to make their escape" with the help of what he called "trustworthy and Patriotic colored men." In short order, Douglass reported back to the president that "All with whom, I have thus far spoken on the subject, concur in the wisdom and benevolence of the idea, and some of them think it is practicable." He then outlined a detailed plan that called for hiring dozens of "agents" at two dollars a day and sending behind enemy lines to visit plantations and encourage slaves to seek refuge. As it turned out, the plan never had to be put into motion. But it certainly demonstrated Lincoln's sincerity as an emancipator. Douglass later agreed that it provided "evidence conclusive on Mr. Lincoln's part that the proclamation, so far at least as he was concerned, was not effected merely as a 'necessity,' but also out of an earnest desire to end human bondage."

When a pro-war Democrat wrote to Lincoln during the campaign to ask whether he would consider asking Jefferson Davis for a truce—perhaps offering to retract the Emancipation Proclamation in return for peace—Lincoln was adamant. The way to restore the Union, he replied, was not "by magic or miracles, but by inducing the colored people to come bodily over from the rebel side to ours." The issues of slavery and freedom no longer remained open to debate. "I am sure you would not desire me to say," wrote Lincoln, " . . . that I am ready, whenever conve-

nient, to join in re-enslaving those who shall have served us in
consideration of our promise. As a matter of morals, could such
treachery by any possibility, escape the curses of Heaven, or of
any good men? As a matter of policy, to *announce* such a purpose,
would ruin the Union cause itself. All recruiting of colored
men would instantly cease, and all colored men now in our service, would instantly desert us. And rightfully too. Why should
they give their lives for us, with full notice of our purpose to
betray them?"

Still, Lincoln sensed that his unbreakable support for emancipation would likely cost him many votes in November. He still
believed he had little chance of reelection until a major military
success suddenly reversed the political momentum. On September 2, three days after the Democrats nominated McClellan to
oppose Lincoln for president, General William T. Sherman captured the city of Atlanta. Then Sherman commenced a dramatic
march to the Atlantic shore. Lincoln proudly declared that the
general's triumph would live forever "in the annals of war," and
offered the "applause and thanks of the nation" to "those who
have participated." The stunning Union victory proved a political game-changer.

Lincoln now began to believe he might just squeak through
the election contest after all. When the votes were counted on
November 8, he received almost 56 percent of the total—a near-
landslide. In the all-important Electoral College, Lincoln won
overwhelmingly, with 212 votes to McClellan's 21. It turned
out to be one of the most lopsided triumphs in American history. Perhaps most gratifying of all to the president, the soldiers'
votes, counted separately in the days before absentee ballots,

favored Lincoln most heavily of all. Even though McClellan had once been a popular commander among his men, the president overwhelmingly defeated him among the troops, 80 to 20 percent.

Mary Lincoln was especially relieved by the news. She had run up many unpaid bills in her growing mania to buy clothing for herself and decorations like velvet curtains and fancy dishes for the White House. She had come to live in fear that if her husband lost the election, he would find out about the debts and, worse, be required to pay them. Victory or not, Mary remained worried, this time about the president's declining vitality. For the first time in their twenty-three years as husband and wife, Mary thought Lincoln had begun to look older than his years. As she admitted in fear to her confidante Lizzie Keckly, "Poor Mr. Lincoln is looking so broken-hearted, so completely worn out, I fear he will not get through the next four years."

But an overjoyed Lincoln felt reenergized by his victory. He regarded his reelection as proof the Union was willing after all to fight for freedom. To a crowd that gathered on election night outside the White House, Lincoln declared that his reelection provided strong "evidence of the people's resolution to stand by free government and the rights of humanity."

With the people so strongly behind him, Lincoln quickly turned to making the promise of the Union Party platform a reality: the great work of passing a constitutional amendment banning slavery. The country Lincoln had once called a "house divided" was perhaps close at last to reuniting under the banner of liberty.

For a time, however, Lincoln worried that his own house remained divided, too. For months, his son Robert had tried to convince his father that he should be allowed to enlist in the army. So many young men his age had served—and died—in military service, and several of Robert's Harvard classmates had gone to war. The president's son had a point: other families were suffering far more hardships in defense of the Union, and to many it seemed unfair that Lincoln's own adult child had not joined the ranks. Some of Lincoln's political enemies whispered that the president received special preference for his own child, a charge that only made Robert more eager to sign up.

Lincoln withheld his approval for one reason only: he believed that if Robert died in battle, his fragile wife Mary would fall over an emotional cliff and lose her reason entirely. She had already seen two of her sons die, and now lived in perpetual fear that something terrible would happen to Robert or Tad. Lincoln felt he had enough on his hands without worrying about further risking his wife's health, and he begged Robert to understand. Meanwhile, he gently prepared Mary for the fact that like other sons, Robert would eventually have to serve, too.

"I know that Robert's plea to go into the Army is manly and noble," Mary moaned to her husband at one point, "and I want him to go, but oh! I am so frightened he may never come back to me."

After Robert graduated from Harvard College in 1864 and entered Harvard Law School, the boy increased the pressure on his father to give him permission to enlist—permission that, as an adult, he technically no longer needed. "Many a poor mother, Mary, has had to make this sacrifice and has given up every son she had—and lost them all," Lincoln reminded his wife. Finally, the president hit upon a plan. Two months before his scheduled inauguration, he wrote a private letter to General Grant proposing that he take Robert onto his personal staff. Asking that Grant decide the question "as though I was not President, but only a friend," Lincoln explained: "My son, now in his twenty second year, having graduated at Harvard, wishes to see something of the war before it ends. I do not wish to put him in the ranks, nor yet to give him a commission, to which those who have already served long, are better entitled, and better qualified to hold. Could he, without embarrassment to you, or detriment to the service, go into your Military family with some nominal rank, I, and not the public, furnishing his necessary means?" A few days later, Grant graciously replied that he would be "most happy" to add the young man to his official staff. General Grant awarded him the rank of captain. And Robert T. Lincoln, as he preferred to be called, headed off at last to fight for his country, his father, and freedom.

CHAPTER THIRTEEN

A FITTING AND NECESSARY CONCLUSION

The campaign for the new Thirteenth Amendment had begun even before Lincoln launched his own campaign for a second term as president.

In January 1864, Senator John B. Henderson of Missouri—a pro-war Democrat—submitted the first congressional resolution calling for a constitutional amendment outlawing slavery. Members of the Senate Judiciary Committee started working on the draft, with President Lincoln's old Illinois colleague Lyman Trumbull in the lead. As they labored over the language of the proposal, members of Congress began considering, too, a crucial and thorny procedural question. The law required that two-thirds of each body, both House and Senate, approve the constitutional amendment. But did this mean two-thirds of those Northern and Border State legislators actually serving at the time in Congress—a supermajority that might be possible? Or did it mean two-thirds of all who were *elected* and legally *entitled* to serve, including the senators who had abruptly resigned their seats at the onset of the secession crisis? No one believed it was possible to pass the resolution if it needed a two-thirds vote of the Senate as it was before the war. Eventually, the House and Senate majorities—that is, the Republicans—simply declared that passage would require approval only by two-thirds of those seated and voting. This milestone ruling vastly improved the odds for passage.

That same month, Illinois Congressman Isaac N. Arnold visited Lincoln at the White House and offered his New Year's wishes:

"I hope, Mr. President, that on next New Year's Day I have the pleasure of congratulating you on three events which now seem very probable."

"What are they?"

"First, that the war may be ended by the complete triumph of the Union forces. Second, that slavery may be abolished and prohibited throughout the Union by an amendment to the Constitution. Third, that Abraham Lincoln may have been reelected president."

To which Lincoln replied with a smile, "I think, my friend, I would be willing to accept the first two by way of compromise."

Meanwhile, committee members worked to craft a simple resolution on which as many of them as possible could agree. This meant it would not deal with the dicey subject of "equality before the law," as pro-abolitionist senators like Charles Sumner of Massachusetts hoped. The resolution would only ban "involuntary servitude." The agreed-upon final resolution was straightforward—not enough for some, and perhaps too much for others. Still, even the senators who proposed this simple act of justice felt they were taking a giant step for humanity, and a risky one for their own careers:

SECTION 1. Neither slavery nor involuntary servitude, except as a punishment for crime whereof the party shall have been duly convicted, shall exist within the United States, or any place subject to their jurisdiction.

SECTION 2. Congress shall have the power to enforce this article by appropriate legislation.

That April, a full two months before the Republican convention was scheduled to begin, Congress began engaging in on-the-record discussions of the proposal on the House and Senate floors. At this historic moment, surprisingly, it was the Republican group that backed down. Like the president, many were facing reelection that fall. They feared that voters at home would turn against them and turn them out of office if they did anything that changed the status of African Americans. While Republicans hesitated, members of the Democratic Party unexpectedly began speaking out in favor of the amendment. Slavery was dying anyway, one of them pointed out. Why should the Democrats continue to support it? Could the party not gain far more influence by going with the tide, instead of against it?

From a purely political point of view, Democrats began to imagine that if they successfully seized the slavery issue away from the Republicans, they would have a far greater chance of winning back majorities in the House and Senate, and perhaps the presidency, too. Some abolitionists feared that the

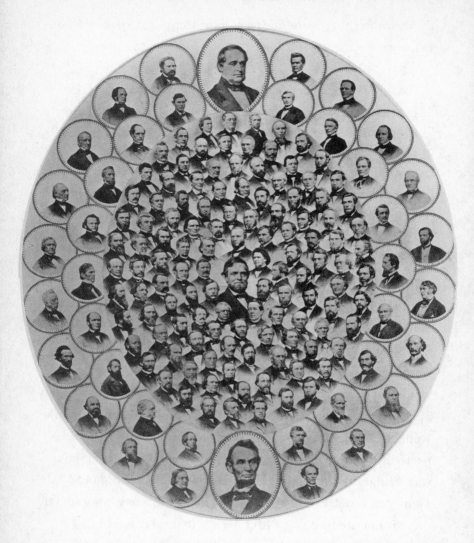

Americans of the day never doubted that Lincoln had pushed for the constitutional end of slavery. This montage of portraits entitled Congressional Supporters of the Thirteenth Amendment *showed Lincoln in a prominent position on the bottom, even though he was not a member of Congress. (Courtesy Lincoln Financial Foundation Collection, Indiana State Museum, Ref. # 2603)*

Democrats were only pretending to favor the amendment, and would very likely overturn it once they won back the White House. Lincoln's closest allies in Congress worried, too, that if the Democrats rallied behind the issue, the president would lose the credit he deserved as an emancipator. But all friends of freedom cheered when, in a dramatic development, Border State Democratic Senator Reverdy Johnson came out eloquently in favor of the amendment. "I never doubted," he said, "the day must one day come when human slavery must be terminated." The *Chicago Tribune* cheered: "We doubt if the rebel cause has got a harder blow since Vicksburg was taken than it got in the Senate when Reverdy Johnson laid his blows." The very next day, his home state of Maryland announced it would hold a convention to consider a measure of its own banning slavery. The tide was turning.

In the end, however, it was not to be a truly bipartisan effort. Incurable racism stopped additional congressional Democrats from embracing Johnson's approach. As one party spokesman insisted, "to free [the slaves] would be an act of cruelty to the race compared with which their actual extermination would be a blessing." After the brief Democratic bubble for freedom burst, its original supporters concluded that the amendment faced a long fight and an uncertain future after all.

While all this political maneuvering was playing out, antislavery Republicans resumed urging Lincoln to add his voice to those of the progressives who sincerely wanted slavery killed for nobler reasons. But until the Republican convention that June, Lincoln remained publicly silent on the issue. Why did Lincoln hold his tongue for so long? One explanation is that he had already exercised unheard-of presidential power to declare emancipation. Now he needed Congress to act, too—on its own, if necessary—to create the permanent constitutional authority to keep emancipation from being overturned. Moreover, he did not want freedom to become a political football in the coming presidential campaign. Keeping his silence was a big political risk. But for three years Lincoln had shown that he was the smartest politician in town. He seemed to know exactly when to act, and precisely when to "hide." At this moment, he hid.

When formal debate actually got underway, however, Johnson's bold change of heart failed to persuade his Democratic colleagues, or free them from their fear of black equality. "This Government was made by white men and for white men," railed an angry Senator Lazarus Powell, "and if it is ever preserved it must be preserved by white men." Opponents began a whispering campaign suggesting that the amendment was merely a first step toward racial equality and intermarriage. Even some Republicans hesitated because of the "equality" controversy. Other opponents argued that the nation's founders had clearly endorsed the slave system, and that even if their wishes could be reversed, or modified, it was up to the states, not the federal government, to do the changing. Supporters like Senator Thomas Shannon of California countered by arguing that ending slavery forever would remove the evil that caused the bloody war in the first place. It would, as he put it, destroy "the root of the accursed tree."

On April 7, 1864, visitors crowded the Senate galleries to overflowing so they could witness what promised to be a historic moment. The upper chamber of Congress was ready at last to

vote on the Thirteenth Amendment. When the presiding officer called the roll, forty-four members answered "present." This
meant that thirty "aye" votes would be needed for the required
two-thirds majority of those in their seats. Slowly the senators'
names were called again. When the counting was done, thirty-
eight had voted yes, and only six no. The measure had soundly
passed in the U.S. Senate!

Not a single Republican senator voted against the Thirteenth
Amendment, and a few Democrats, Maryland's influential
Johnson included, crossed the aisle to vote for it. Willard Saulsbury of Delaware, who had once called President Lincoln the
"weakest man ever placed in high office," was among the Democrats who remained bitterly opposed. "I now bid farewell to any
hope of the reconstruction of the American Union," he angrily
declared before the Senate adjourned. Few were surprised by his
fury. A year earlier, Saulsbury had launched such a verbal attack against Lincoln so vicious that the Senate sergeant at arms
approached his seat to remove him forcibly from the floor—at
which point the bellicose senator took out a pistol and threat-
ened to shoot him!

But as political observers noted, the Senate had acted this day
without any formal instructions from Lincoln. With the Republican convention only a few more weeks away, the president still
wanted to keep his distance from the hot and divisive issue. "I
claim not to have controlled events," he modestly insisted around
this time, "but confess plainly that events have controlled me.
Now, at the end of three years struggle the nation's condition
is not what either party, or any man devised, or expected. God
alone can claim it. Whither it is tending seems plain. If God

now wills the removal of a great wrong, and wills also that we of the North as well as you of the South, shall pay fairly for our complicity in that wrong, impartial history will find therein new cause to attest and revere the justice and goodness of God."

The president's message could not have been clearer. God had influenced Lincoln, and in return Lincoln had influenced history. Emancipation and the organization of the U.S. Colored Troops followed. And now the amendment was next on God's agenda. Lincoln still avoided venturing his own personal opinions about the measure. But he was suggesting his own views did not matter. *God* wanted it passed.

The House of Representatives took up the amendment question on May 31. Though Lincoln again refrained from stating his personal preference, when his party's convention convened a few days later, he instructed his spokesman to make sure that the keystone in the party's platform supported the constitutional amendment that would abolish and prohibit slavery forever. On June 15, the House of Representatives got its chance to do exactly that, but failed. The final House vote was ninety-three for the amendment and sixty-five against—a majority, to be sure, but not enough. It was thirteen votes short of the two-thirds needed for passage. Twenty-three members had made sure they were absent for the roll call, and one abstained. For now, the measure was dead. Lincoln's hope of keeping the constitutional amendment issue out of the presidential campaign died, too. The real vote would come, after all, on Election Day. Freedom advocates quickly changed their focus and turned their attention to Lincoln's race for president. Only if he won reelection would the final nail be hammered into the coffin of slavery.

Lincoln struggled to save his presidency. Not everyone in 1864 applauded his sense of justice and humanity. In the darkest days of the heated, ugly campaign, as the Democrats relentlessly hammered away at Lincoln as a friend of integration and race-mixing, the president was briefly forced, by some accounts, to consider peace without freedom. The *New York Times* urged Lincoln to send a delegation to Richmond to offer a peace deal to the Confederacy, or face losing the presidency to McClellan. But Lincoln held firm to his promise; he would not now compromise on freedom.

Perhaps the most heartening day in the entire campaign came on September 8, when a group from Baltimore calling itself a "Committee of Colored Men" arrived at the White House to present Lincoln with a Bible in "appreciation of your humane conduct towards the people of our race." The inscription read, "To Abraham Lincoln, President of the United States, the Friend of Universal Freedom, from the Loyal Colored People of Baltimore, as a token of respect and Gratitude." Deeply moved, Lincoln could only bring himself to respond, "[A]s I have often before said, it has always been a sentiment with me that all mankind should be free. So far as able, I have always acted as I believed to be right and just."

Lincoln's huge Election Day victory signified for him that the people accepted and supported emancipation. One month later, in December, he used his Annual Message to Congress to herald the vote as "the voice of the people now, for the first time, heard on the question" of freedom. "May we not agree the sooner the better?" he asked. "Unanimity of action among those seeking a common end is desirable." Now he was ready to make "the voice of the people" heard nationwide. Over the next five months, he did all he could—and more than any president before him—to win complete freedom for African Americans.

More hope arrived that fall as well. In mid-October, Chief Justice Taney died at the age of eighty-seven after serving decades on the Supreme Court and years fighting the black man's claim to freedom and equality. Lincoln waited until after his reelection to propose a successor, but when he announced his choice on December 6, many Americans expressed surprise. Lincoln chose a man for whom he had no personal affection—someone who had treated him with selfishness and disloyalty. His selection was none other than former Secretary of the Treasury Salmon P. Chase, who just a few months earlier had shamelessly tried to replace Lincoln as the Republican candidate for president. Despite their adversary relationship, Lincoln knew he could trust Chase to vote to uphold emancipation if its legality ever came before the Supreme Court. Chase was no friend of Lincoln, but he was a friend of black freedom, and that was enough for the remarkably selfless president. Once he announced the Chase appointment, Lincoln turned back to the major challenge at hand: a new vote in the House of Representatives on the Thirteenth Amendment.

Many wondered then—and some have wondered since—why Lincoln did not simply wait until the next Congress convened in Washington the following year before reinstituting his campaign for the amendment. After all, if he had allowed newly chosen House and Senate members to take their seats, both chambers would have been overwhelmingly Republican and the amendment would have easily won support of the two-thirds needed.

The amendment would easily have won the next two-thirds test in the next House of Representatives, where the effort had fallen thirteen short during the June vote. The president could have called this new Congress into session right after his next inauguration, in March 1865. Or he might have waited until the summer, for another dramatic July 4 session like the one four years earlier at which he had defended his power to fight the rebellion. Independence Day 1865 would have been a perfect symbolic moment to extend independence to the millions who had been denied it in the eighty-nine years since the founding of the country.

Instead, the president decided to push the amendment as soon as possible through the same House of Representatives that had previously voted *not* to support it. For one thing, he reasoned that prompter passage would not only liberate people sooner, but could also save the lives of soldiers and reunite the country more quickly. Every day the war continued hundreds, even thousands, more died fighting for the Union cause. Every day that slavery remained legal, millions remained in chains, subject to forced labor and inhumane cruelty.

But as usual, politics also played a role in Lincoln's strategy for speed. Some of the current members of the House would not be returning for the next Congress. These "lame ducks," as they were called, no longer need fear that voters would defeat them if they defied tradition and voted for freedom. In a sense, by losing their elections, they had freed themselves to act according to their conscience. And they still had a few weeks to serve out their terms.

Then there was the political diplomacy at play. Lincoln did

not want to see the Emancipation Proclamation come up as a bargaining chip in any discussion he might have with the South over peace. As long as emancipation remained only an order by the president, Lincoln worried that Confederates might offer to suspend the fighting, even rejoin the Union, if in return he agreed to cancel freedom. Jefferson Davis had never actually asked for such a deal, but what if he did? Would the Northern people, exhausted by war, death, and destruction, support further combat? Lincoln worried they might not. He decided that the subject of freedom must be taken out of his own hands and attached at last to the Constitution so he could *not* be asked to sacrifice liberty for peace.

To take emancipation off the table, Lincoln urgently needed the House to act again, quickly and positively, on the amendment it had rejected earlier in the year. He believed that his big victory on Election Day gave him the power and influence to make the request—and to force at least thirteen more congressmen to listen and bend to his will. How Lincoln proceeded to win those reluctant votes proved a testament to his almost ruthless determination to achieve the goal of freedom so he could pursue the goal of peace without slavery.

First, even before Election Day, he pushed Congress to admit a new state to the Union, Nevada. The southwestern territory was solidly Republican and would surely send new Republican congressmen to the House in time for the lame-duck winter session. Lincoln wanted them seated immediately in order to provide additional votes for the amendment. When the House resumed business in December, Nevada was safely in the Union and its new delegation was in Washington for the

renewed debate. Lincoln also held a secret White House meeting with a wealthy New Yorker named Abel R. Corbin. This
financier had strong connections to his state's congressional
delegation. Ever on the lookout for deals that would profit him
later, Corbin offered to persuade some of his anti-amendment
friends to switch their votes—or at least arrange not to be present to vote no next time the amendment came up—in return
for future favors from the president. Lincoln swallowed hard
but accepted the deal. Then Corbin went further, suggesting he
could also sway the votes of two Missouri congressmen opposed
to the amendment, August King and James S. Rollins, a major
slaveholder. All Lincoln had to do was take their advice about
an important upcoming presidential appointment: that of a federal judgeship in their home state. By the time Lincoln discussed
the matter directly with Congressman Rollins, the Missourian
was ready to say he would change his vote to yes and work on
securing King's support as well. Just as Lincoln hoped, both
men ended up supporting the amendment. Whether Lincoln
actually traded away a judgeship in return for their votes we do
not really know for sure, but he probably would have done so if
needed.

Lincoln next welcomed two more important Democratic
congressmen to the White House to talk about the amendment:
Samuel "Sunset" Cox of Ohio and none other than John Todd
Stuart of Illinois—Mary Lincoln's beloved cousin and the president's first law partner thirty years earlier. It was Stuart who,
decades before, had first urged the young Lincoln to take up the
study of the law. But politics had come to divide them. Stuart
was now an anti-emancipation member of the political opposi-

tion, and though he had visited the White House often during his cousin-in-law's presidency, the two old friends remained divided on the issue of freedom. On Election Day a few weeks earlier, Stuart had lost his seat in Congress to a Republican. He was now back in Washington to serve out his term as a lame duck. Lincoln's two visitors that day came on a mission of their own. During their visit, Cox and Stuart asked Lincoln to be more aggressive in seeking peace talks with Jefferson Davis. Lincoln listened and then shifted the conversation. He wanted their support for the amendment. He would make a "sincere effort" to negotiate peace, he promised, if the two men would change their votes. But the promise was not enough for Lincoln's own cousin-in-law. John Todd Stuart voted against the Thirteenth Amendment every chance he got.

On and on Lincoln worked, grabbing yes votes one by one wherever he could. To two more congressmen who seemed to be wavering, Lincoln said, "I leave it to you to determine how it shall be done; but remember that I am President of the United States and clothed with great power, and I expect you to procure those votes." And to yet another member of the House whose own brother had lost his life in the Civil War, Lincoln said: "[Y]our brother died to save the Republic from death by the slaveholders' rebellion. I wish you could see it to be your duty to vote for the constitutional amendment ending slavery." When New York Democrat Anson Herrick admitted that he feared he would be punished by his party at home if he voted for the amendment, Lincoln probably promised to ease the pain by offering a federal job for Herrick's brother. (After the vote, Lincoln in fact ordered that the promise be "fulfilled," but the president died before the appointment could be confirmed by the Senate, and Herrick's brother never got his reward after all.)

Perhaps the most shocking of the Lincoln administration's maneuvers to secure passage of the amendment may have come when the president—or his friends in Congress—tried to persuade antislavery Senator Charles Sumner to drop a bill he had introduced to break up a railroad monopoly in New Jersey. There was no question that the existing railroad system was corrupt. But freedom advocates whispered to Sumner that if he abandoned or postponed his effort to regulate the railroad system, he might shake loose several more votes for the amendment from New Jersey's congressional delegation. For decades thereafter, Washington insiders whispered that Lincoln had agreed to the bargain, though, as the president suspected, Sumner did not. All that anti-slavery Congressman Thaddeus Stevens would later admit was that while Sumner refused to take the deal, enough fellow senators withdrew their support for the railroad bill to win backing for the slavery amendment from New Jersey. In Stevens's view, the Thirteenth Amendment "was passed by corruption, aided and abetted by the purest man in America"—the president of the United States.

One last obstacle remained to winning the two-thirds majority needed for passage in the House of Representatives. Both political parties wanted peace, and Lincoln had spent weeks making the case to Democrats that he could not discuss a truce with the Confederates unless Congress took the emancipation issue out of his hands to prevent it from becoming a negotiating point. Then, just as the congressional debate was winding down at the end of January 1865, word reached the capital that three

Confederate leaders were on their way to Washington to propose peace immediately. The so-called "Peace Commissioners" included Alexander H. Stephens himself, vice president of the Confederacy and Lincoln's onetime colleague when both served together in Congress.

Angry Democrats fumed that Lincoln was trying to have it both ways, peace and freedom alike. Several of them declared they would refuse to vote in favor of the amendment if peace talks were really going to occur at any moment. House Democrats demanded that Lincoln either confirm or deny the rumor.

Fearing the crisis would destroy the careful work of two difficult months, Congressman James M. Ashley, the legislator who had introduced the amendment resolution in the House, sent a worried note to the president: "The report is in circulation in the House that Peace Commissioners are on their way or are in the city, and it is being used against us. If it is true, I fear we shall lose the bill. Please authorize me to contradict it, if not true." It was then that "Honest Abe" dashed off a reply that, if not totally dishonest, was at least not completely true. As the president well knew, the three Confederate peace emissaries had been stopped at City Point, Virginia. They would be held there pending further instructions. So Lincoln could confidently write the following reply, "So far as I know, there are no peace commissioners in this city"—meaning Washington—"or likely to be in it." Congressman "Sunset" Cox, for one, did not believe the president. The rumors were enough to persuade him to vote no on the amendment. Indeed, he was right about his doubts. Just a few days later, Lincoln headed off to Virginia to see the three Peace Commissioners at City Point. The president had not exactly lied. But he had used words craftily enough to save the Thirteenth Amendment.

On January 31, 1865, an immense crowd of men and women packed the House visitors' gallery to watch the scheduled voting. No one on the scene was absolutely certain how the vote would go, though nearly everybody realized it would depend on who showed up to cast their ballots—and who did not. Visitors and congressmen alike surely noticed at once that a prominent anti-amendment Democrat from New Jersey failed to appear. "Confined to his room" by a supposed illness, he would be unable to vote no. With 183 House members present, 122 would have to say "aye" to secure passage of the resolution. But eight members cast no vote at all, reducing the required "ayes" to 110. Now there was support to spare. To wild cheering from the galleries, the clerk announced the final vote of 119 to 56. The *New York Times* called the response from the galleries "grand and responsive beyond description." Congressman George Julian of Indiana hailed the vote as "one of the grandest events of the century."

Not a single Republican had voted no, and seventeen Democrats had joined them to guarantee passage—thirteen more than in the 1864 vote. "If by my action, I dig my political grave," Congressman Alexander Coffroth, a Democrat from Pennsylvania, told his colleagues, "I will descend into it without a murmur knowing I am justified and that I am doing what will ultimately prove to be a service to my country." Coffroth and the other Democrats who broke ranks to support freedom indeed ended up paying the heavy price they feared. Nearly all the border-

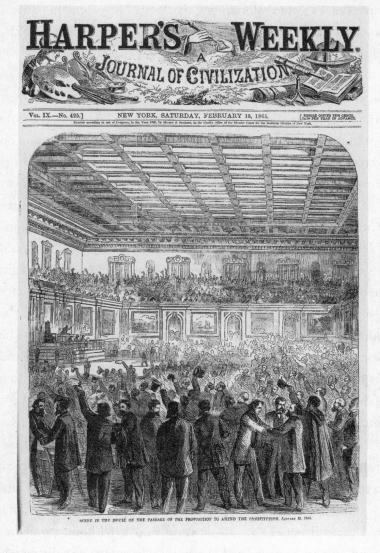

SCENE IN THE HOUSE ON THE PASSAGE OF THE PROPOSITION TO AMEND THE CONSTITUTION, January 31, 1865.

Congress erupts in celebration as the House of Representatives votes to send the Thirteenth Amendment to the states on January 31, 1865. This sketch was made on the scene for Frank Leslie's Illustrated Newspaper. *(Courtesy Lincoln Financial Foundation Collection, Indiana State Museum, Ref. #4610)* state congressmen who supported the Thirteenth Amendment that day lost their seats in the next election.

But Lincoln was elated. Whether or not he really dirtied his own hands making bargains to secure passage of the amendment we still do not know for sure. But if he did, the president would have defended his actions to the death. Freedom had already cost some six hundred thousand lives North and South. If it cost a bit more in deals, promises, jobs, and threats, the result was well worth the price.

So Lincoln believed when he appeared at the White House window to celebrate passage with his speech to the crowd of joyous citizens who gathered outside. So he had felt when he enthusiastically signed his name to a document that did not technically require his signature for approval. The amendment was already on its way to the states for passage. And Lincoln would soon be on his way to Hampton Roads, Virginia, to negotiate for peace—perhaps, he prayed, to "wind the whole thing up" at last.

Before the end of February, legislatures in eighteen of the twenty-seven states required for ratification of the amendment had quickly vote to support it, in this order: Illinois, Rhode Island, Michigan, Maryland, New York, Pennsylvania, West Virginia, Missouri, Maine, Massachusetts, Kansas, Virginia (the first onetime Confederate state to ratify), Ohio, Indiana, Nevada, Louisiana (the second former Confederate state to approve), Minnesota, and Wisconsin.

In March and April three more states ratified: Vermont, Tennessee, and the no longer Confederate state of Arkansas. Sadly, Lincoln was dead by the time the twenty-seventh state—Georgia—ratified the Thirteenth Amendment to make it part of the Constitution. And while he lived, some states remained stubbornly opposed. Delaware voted no on February 12, Lincoln's fifty-sixth, and last, birthday. Mississippi voted no in March, as did the president's birth state of Kentucky—a bitter disappointment to him.

Some former Confederate states did not approve the Thirteenth Amendment until long after it became law. Delaware at least came around with belated, symbolic ratification in 1901. Kentucky did so in 1976. Mississippi took 130 years to offer its support. Its legislature did not vote to ratify until 1995!

CHAPTER FOURTEEN

DEATH OF A LIBERATOR

A s it turned out, neither the constitutional amendment nor the Hampton Roads peace talks ended the Civil War as quickly as Abraham Lincoln desired. Hoping for a breakthrough, the president had decided to travel to Virginia to confer with the Confederate negotiators himself. "Say to the gentlemen I will meet them personally at Fortress-Monroe, as soon as I can get there," Lincoln telegraphed General Grant before leaving Washington on February 2. Grant was one of the few leaders told about the meeting. Otherwise, the trip remained top secret.

On the morning of February 3, Lincoln and Secretary of State Seward began four hours of discussions with the three "Rebel Commissioners" on board the presidential steamship *River Queen*. No one kept a record of the discussion. One thing we do know for sure: The Confederate commissioners came to the conference prepared to offer peace in return for slavery. But Lincoln insisted on what he called "indispensable" conditions:

the Confederate states must recognize federal authority; there would be no pause in hostilities "short of an end of the war, and the disbanding of all forces hostile to the government"; and, perhaps most important of all, he would tolerate no "receding on the Slavery question." The message was clear: Abraham Lincoln would not trade black freedom for peace.

Once Seward also informed the peace commissioners that the House of Representatives had just passed the resolution sending the Thirteenth Amendment to the states for ratification, the negotiations all but collapsed. The secret peace conference ended in failure, but in a way, slavery itself ended that day, too. Faced with one of the biggest decisions of his life, Lincoln would not compromise on freedom.

When Lincoln returned to the White House, he took up an equally important task: the writing of his second inaugural address, scheduled for the following month. Conditions looked better. The peace conference may have failed, but Union forces under Grant were succeeding against Lee's starving Confederates in Virginia. The rebellion looked doomed, and the end might finally be near. Under the circumstances, Lincoln might easily have used his March 4 inaugural address to take credit for the approaching victory. But he did not. Instead, in one of the most remarkable speeches of his entire life, Lincoln did the unexpected—he asked Northerners to share blame for the war. Instead of stressing the fact that Northerners had long *opposed* slavery, he pointed to the fact that they had too long *accepted* it. There was more than enough guilt to go around. And if God meant the war to continue until all the guilty were punished for their sins, North as well as South, then Lincoln warned that the bloodletting would continue. For the first time, the audience that gathered outside the Capitol for a presidential inaugural was fully integrated. Black and white people alike listened to the striking words that seemed to accept the tragic reality of war while looking to a future of peace. This is how he concluded what was perhaps his greatest oration:

Fondly do we hope—fervently do we pray—that this mighty scourge of war may speedily pass away. Yet, if God wills that it continue until all the wealth piled by the bondman's two hundred and fifty years of unrequited toil shall be sunk, and until every drop of blood drawn with the lash, shall be paid by another drawn with the sword, as was said three thousand years ago, so still it must be said, "the judgments of the Lord are true and righteous altogether."

With malice toward none; with charity for all; with firmness in the right, as God gives us to see the right, let us strive on to finish the work we are in; to bind up the nation's wounds; to care for him who shall have borne the battle, and for his widow, and his orphan—to do all which may achieve and cherish, a just and a lasting peace, among ourselves, and with all nations.

As usual, Republicans and Democrats differed radically in their responses to Lincoln's speech. The pro-Lincoln *Washington Intelligencer* declared that its concluding paragraph deserved "to be printed in gold." But the anti-Lincoln *Chicago Times* called the oration "slip-shod." Lincoln himself worried that it was "not immediately popular." As he admitted, "Men are not flattered

Lincoln delivers his second inaugural address from the U. S. Capitol, March 4, 1865, as seen in a photograph by Alexander Gardner. (Courtesy Library of Congress)

by being shown that there has been a difference of purpose between the Almighty and them." Nonetheless, Lincoln still expected the speech "to wear as well as—perhaps better than—any thing I have produced."

One observer who brought a distinct point of view to Lincoln's performance was Frederick Douglass, who attended the ceremonies as a guest. When it was over, Douglass headed to the White House for a post-inaugural reception. But guards there refused at first to permit an African American to join the all-white event. Not to be deterred, Douglass pushed his way inside and made his way toward the president's side. Glimpsing him as he approached, Lincoln's face "lighted up" and he startled his conservative guests by loudly announcing, "Here comes my friend Douglass." The abolitionist leader never forgot what happened next:

> As I approached him he reached out his hand, gave me a cordial shake, and said: "Douglass, I saw you in the crowd to-day listening to my inaugural address. There is no man's opinion that I value more than yours: what did you think of it?" I said: "Mr. Lincoln, I cannot stop here to talk with you, as there are thousands waiting to shake you by the hand"; but he said again: "What did you think of it?" I said: "Mr. Lincoln, it was a sacred effort," and then I walked off. "I am glad you liked it," he said. That was the last time I saw him.

A few days later, feeling more relaxed at last, Lincoln decided that he wanted to be on hand in Virginia for what he hoped would be the end of the war. On March 23, the president, Mary, and Tad took a boat to visit Grant's army in Virginia. Robert had briefly visited Washington for the inauguration, but had since returned to the army, and his parents planned to see him when they reached headquarters. Though Lincoln stayed with Grant

for more than two weeks, Mary had an embarrassing public out-
burst midway through their stay and returned to Washington.
While she was back at the White House, Lincoln reported that
he had enjoyed a four-hour reunion with Bob, who seemed "well
& in good spirits." Missing her husband and children, Mary
asked if she could return to Virginia. "Tad and I are both well,"
the president replied, "and will be glad to see you."

Unfortunately for her, Mary was not yet back on the scene
when news reached Lincoln and Grant that the Confederate government had fled from Richmond. Union forces had marched in
without opposition and now occupied the onetime enemy capital. Overjoyed, Lincoln resolved to visit the city—"I want to see
Richmond," he told Admiral David Dixon Porter—even though
Porter, Grant, and others worried for his safety there.

On April 4—Tad's twelfth birthday—Lincoln set out by ship
for the conquered city with twelve sailors and marines as his only
guards. Because "torpedoes," or mines, still filled the surrounding waters, the presidential party was forced to transfer twice to
successively smaller boats. By the time the group reached land,
the leader of what had become, militarily, the mightiest nation
in the world was riding in a modest rowboat. Lincoln and Tad
stepped ashore and began walking up a hill, the acrid smell of
smoke filling their nostrils as they strolled, for the Confederates
had set fire to much of the town before escaping. Richmond was
in ruins, still smoldering.

Near the riverbank, a group of African American workers
could be seen laboring in the broiling sun. They probably knew
already that once the Union Army entered Richmond, they were
legally free under the terms of the Emancipation Proclamation.

But they surely never expected to see the proclamation's author up close. Once the workers realized who was approaching them, these former slaves rushed excitedly toward the president and began kissing his hand, crying, and shouting with joy. "Bless the Lord," they yelled as they surrounded the visitor, " . . . there is the great Messiah! Glory, Hallelujah!"

One elderly man fell to his knees to thank the man he considered his deliverer. Now in tears himself, Lincoln urged him

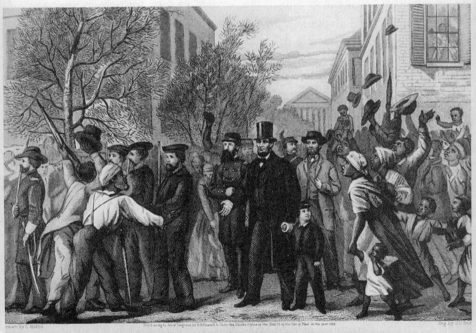

ABRAHAM LINCOLN ENTERING RICHMOND, APRIL 3ᴰ 1865
PUBLISHED BY B.B.RUSSELL & CO. BOSTON

Printmaker B. B. Russell imagined how the scene looked when Lincoln and his son, Tad, arrived to tour conquered Richmond, Virginia, on April 4, 1865—where the president was joyously greeted by newly freed African Americans. (Courtesy Library of Congress)

to rise. "Don't kneel to me, that is not right," he gently told him. "You must kneel to God only, and thank him for the liberty you will hereafter enjoy." News of Lincoln's arrival spread rapidly. Even as the old gentleman rose to his feet, hundreds of African Americans began rushing to the scene, "tumbling and shouting, from over the hills and from the water-side," said one eyewitness, "to see the man they believed to be their liberator and friend." When one black gentleman lifted his battered hat and tipped it to the president with a grand bow, Lincoln returned the gesture of respect. He doffed his own stovepipe topper—perhaps the first time an American president had ever tipped his hat to a black man. From behind their windows on the upper floors of the surrounding houses, white women looked on in anger and disgust. As Lincoln later admitted, his enemies could easily have killed him that day.

"Abraham Lincoln was their Savior, their Moses," remembered a reporter about the greeting Lincoln enjoyed from Richmond's African Americans that day. One elderly woman declared, "I know that I am free, for I have seen Father Abraham and felt him." Lincoln had met few actual slaves during his presidency. On this historic day, however, the president finally got to experience firsthand the human impact of what he had once described only as a "military order." The only report Lincoln allowed himself to send to Secretary of State Seward in Washington was a simple telegram: "I passed last night in Richmond and have just returned." In truth, he had passed that April 4 from a mere man to a genuine messiah.

Lincoln soon headed back to Washington. He was not with the army when Robert E. Lee surrendered to Ulysses S. Grant on April 9. In fact, he was still aboard his steamer. But when he docked at sundown, he found Washington ablaze with bonfires, its church bells ringing in celebration. The war was finally over.

The very next evening, a happy crowd massed outside the White House, filling the lawn and driveways. Musicians began serenading the president and calling for him to address them. Lincoln finally made a brief appearance from the usual upstairs window and admitted he felt "greatly rejoiced" that the people could not restrain their happiness. But he insisted he was not ready to make a formal speech—that would come, he promised, from the same spot the very next night. For now, he merely made a special request for a favorite old piece of music. "I have always thought 'Dixie' one of the best tunes I have ever heard," he declared. "Our adversaries over the way attempted to appropriate it, but I insisted yesterday that we fairly captured it. I presented the question to the Attorney General, and he gave it as his legal opinion that it is our lawful prize. I now request the band to favor me with its performance." And to laughter and applause, the song that for four years had served as a Confederate national anthem was heard again at the White House.

The following night, as promised, Lincoln reappeared in the second-floor White House window to deliver his eagerly awaited answer to the question of what would come next. This time another big audience was on hand also to hear what the president planned to do to reunite the shattered and war-weary country. Lincoln did not offer a particularly eloquent speech that night. Though his mood remained good, he wanted to focus on future challenges, not past glories. But he started his speech by acknowledging the relief in so many Northern hearts. "We meet this evening," he began, "not in sorrow, but in gladness of heart." He predicted "a righteous and speedy peace whose joyous expression cannot be restrained."

And then he turned his attention to the challenging business of the future. He would likely apply the Emancipation Proclamation to those areas in Louisiana and elsewhere that had been exempted from the original order two years earlier. He would oppose forced apprenticeships for freed slaves. But he also wanted Northerners to do all they could to restore Southern states to a "proper practical relation" with the Union. To Lincoln, the Southern states were like lonely travelers who had spent too much time away and now longed to return to where they belonged. "Finding themselves safely at home," he predicted, "it would be utterly immaterial whether they had ever been abroad."

Then Lincoln dropped a political bombshell—his first comments on the hot topic of civil rights for free African Americans. "It is also unsatisfactory to some," he began, "that the elective franchise is not given to the colored man. I myself would prefer that it were now conferred on the very intelligent, and on those who serve in our cause as soldiers."

To modern ears, these tentative words about black voting rights hardly sound generous. After all, Lincoln was suggesting that only educated black people and veterans of the army would be enfranchised. But to bigoted white people, even these cautious words seemed shocking almost beyond belief. For the first time, an American president was suggesting that black people were entitled to the right to vote.

One of the shocked and angry whites in the crowd on the

White House lawn that night was a famous young actor who had been nurturing a growing hatred for Lincoln. When the president spoke the words about giving African Americans voting rights, the actor turned to his friend Lewis Powell and fumed: "That means n——r citizenship. Now, by God, I will put him through. That will be the last speech he will ever make." The actor's name was John Wilkes Booth.

For months, Booth and a gang of racist, pro-Confederate conspirators had plotted to kidnap Lincoln during one of his frequent carriage rides outside town. They planned to capture him and hold him for ransom until long-held Confederate prisoners of war could be freed in exchange. If thousands of captured rebel soldiers were returned South, Booth believed, Lee's army would again boast the manpower and energy to fight on. But Lee surrendered before Booth could bring his unlikely scheme to fruition. Now the war was over and Lincoln was proposing citizenship for black people, whom Booth despised. Kidnapping was now too good for the president, whom he considered a dictator. "The hour has come when I must change my plan," Booth concluded. Lincoln and other government leaders would have to be murdered. In the resulting turmoil, surely the South would rise again.

Three days later, on Good Friday, April 14, the owner of Ford's Theatre announced that the president would attend a special performance that night of the English comedy *Our American Cousin*. Holy day or not, Lincoln felt that the best remedy for the long years of tragedy was laughter. At least it was so in his case. He needed "a little rest."

When Booth learned of Lincoln's plans, he determined to

kill him that very evening. The actor knew Ford's Theatre extremely well; he had performed there and remained friendly with its owners and stagehands. No one would try to stop him if he entered the building during a performance. He knew the backstage layout so perfectly he was sure he could make his escape untouched. He knew the play so well he would be able to choose the precise scene—the exact line of dialogue—during which to strike. He knew just when a huge burst of laughter would mask the sound of a gunshot.

While Booth and his coconspirators made their final plans—one was to murder Vice President Johnson, another to kill Secretary of State Seward—the Lincolns enjoyed a particularly pleasant day together. The two spent a leisurely time riding and chatting during a carriage drive through the city. They even took the time to visit the Navy Yard and inspect three Union ironclad warships recently damaged at the battle for Fort Fisher in North Carolina.

Along the way, the Lincolns talked about their future. They would go home someday to live out their years in Illinois. Perhaps they could first visit California, or even the Holy Land. But first, the president wanted his wife to emerge from the long shadow of mourning, just as he hoped the country would as well. "Between the war & the loss of our darling Willie—we have both been very miserable . . ." Lincoln whispered to his wife. "We must *both*, be more cheerful in the future."

When they returned to the White House, Lincoln went back for a time to his desk. The last notes he wrote were a letter to a Union general pledging to work for "a Union of hearts and hands as well as of States," and a pass for a Massachusetts congressman to visit him the next day: "Allow Mr. Ashmun & friend to come in at 9. A. M. to-morrow."

By the time he scribbled those final words, the Lincolns were late for the theater. They rode to Senator Ira Harris's nearby house to pick up their guests for the evening—the senator's daughter Clara and her fiancé Major Henry Rathbone—and then dashed to Ford's, where the play was well underway when they stepped through the doors. Nevertheless, when the actors spied the figure of the tall man in black making his way to the specially arranged presidential box above the stage, they stopped their performance. The band struck up "Hail to the Chief" and the audience erupted into cheers and applause. When Lincoln reached his seat above a beautiful display of red, white, and blue bunting, he bowed and smiled at the ovation. Then he sat down and the play resumed. The last thing some members of the audience remembered was the sight of the president pulling back the drapery on his left so he could peer into the audience. The last thing his guests Miss Harris and Major Rathbone saw was the sight of Lincoln gently taking Mary's hand and holding it in his own.

At around 10:20 p.m., Booth crept into the theater, tiptoed around the balcony just as Lincoln had done, entered the presidential box, and closed the door behind him. Then, just as the audience gave out a roar of laughter at the funny line Booth had been waiting for, he snuck up behind the president and at close range shot him in the back of the head with a small pistol. Before anyone knew what was happening, Booth jumped to the stage below, screamed out the Latin motto of Virginia—*sic semper tyrranis*, which means "thus ever to tyrants"—and raced into the wings and out the theater's back door. Lincoln's face instantly fell for-

The assassination of Abraham Lincoln at Ford's Theatre in Washington on April 14, 1865, as visualized by printmakers Currier & Ives. (Courtesy Library of Congress)

ward. He would never open his eyes again. Around the same time, Lewis Powell pushed his way into William Seward's home and tried to stab him to death in his bed. Another of Booth's gang, George Atzerodt, got cold feet and failed to follow his instructions to kill Andrew Johnson.

Inside Ford's, members of the audience froze in their seats—then erupted in a pandemonium of screaming—when they saw the cloud of smoke rising from the president's box and realized what had happened. A doctor pushed his way to Lincoln's side and examined his wounds, pronouncing him fatally wounded. Then a small group of men gently carried the stricken president out into the crowded street and placed him in the back bedroom of a small boardinghouse just across from the theater. Many men would not have lived even minutes after such an injury. Lincoln lived for nine hours. At 7:22 a.m. the next morning, Abraham Lincoln died, surrounded by a handful of government officials and his son Robert, with Mary in the nearby parlor. He was the first president to be assassinated.

By the time Lincoln's body had been returned to Springfield for burial, he had become more than a successful president and commander in chief—more even than an emancipator. In part because his death occurred so close to Easter Sunday, ministers compared him to Jesus, who, they pointed out, also died for his nation's sins. Because his death came during the Jewish holiday of Passover, rabbis likened him to Moses, who had freed his people from slavery but not lived to see the Promised Land. Almost overnight, Abraham Lincoln became a national saint. The days of partisan politics, controversy, and vicious press criticism ended the moment he died. Thanks to Lincoln, however, freedom would live.

Modern Americans still search for an answer to the question of whether Abraham Lincoln deserves the title "Great Emancipator." Should he be given credit for freeing the slaves by issuing his Emancipation Proclamation and masterminding passage of the Thirteenth Amendment? Despite his modest protests about letting events control his leadership, was he far ahead of the vast majority of Americans on the subjects of freedom and equality? Or was he maddeningly slow to catch up?

Frederick Douglass praised Lincoln as the "black man's president" when he eulogized him in New York shortly after the as-

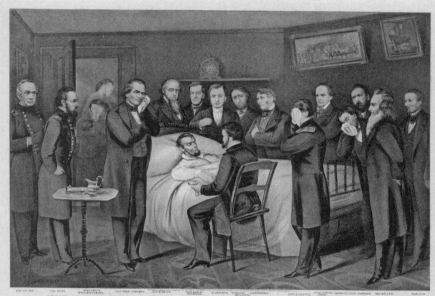

THE DEATH BED OF THE MARTYR PRESIDENT ABRAHAM LINCOLN.
WASHINGTON, SATURDAY MORNING APRIL 15TH 1865, AT 22 MINUTES PAST 7 OYLOCK.

Lincoln's deathbed—another Currier & Ives print. In truth, no artist was present as the president lay dying in a boardinghouse across the street from the theater where he was shot. (Courtesy Library of Congress)

sassination. In the years that followed, however, as Southerners blocked civil rights for black people, Douglass thought harder and longer about the subject. In 1876, he appeared in Washington on the eleventh anniversary of the assassination to speak at the dedication of a memorial statue funded entirely by donations from African Americans. His verdict was mixed. The man he had called the "black man's president" eleven years earlier now seemed to him to have been "preeminently the white man's President, entirely devoted to the welfare of white men."

"You are the children of Abraham Lincoln," he told the whites in the audience. "We are at best only his stepchildren; children by adoption, children by forces of circumstances and necessity."

If Douglass had once resented Lincoln for delaying freedom, now he was at last ready to thank him for ordering it when he did. "Our faith in him was often taxed and strained to the uttermost, but it never failed. . . . It mattered little to us, when we finally knew him, whether he was swift or slow in his movements; it was enough for us that Abraham Lincoln was at the head of a great movement."

Douglass had perhaps finally come to understand the man he had often criticized, and just as often praised. "Viewed from the genuine abolition ground, Mr. Lincoln seemed tardy, cold, dull, and indifferent; but measuring him by the sentiment of his countrymen, a sentiment he was bound as a statesman to consult, he was swift, zealous, radical, and determined." He was, as Douglass concluded that day, and as history has echoed ever since, a liberator.

The last time they had met, Abraham Lincoln had told Frederick Douglass, "I hate slavery as much as you do, and I want to see it abolished altogether." Lincoln died eight months before that dream finally came true with ratification of the Thirteenth Amendment. But he had kept his word to make sure it was abolished "altogether."

Eight *years* earlier, had Lincoln wondered aloud what made American independence special: its power or its promise? It was not, he concluded, "our frowning battlements, our bristling sea coasts, the guns of our war steamers, or the strength of our gallant and disciplined army." After all, he argued, "[a]ll of them may be turned against our liberties, without making us stronger or weaker for the struggle."

"Our reliance is in the *love of liberty* which God has planted in our bosoms."

Thomas Ball's statue Emancipation Group *was unveiled in Lincoln Park, Washington, D.C., on April 15, 1876, the eleventh anniversary of the Lincoln assassination. African Americans raised all the funds for the famous sculpture and Frederick Douglass gave the dedicatory address. (Courtesy Library of Congress)*

APPENDIX

✴ CAST OF CHARACTERS ✴

THE LINCOLN FAMILY
Abraham Lincoln (1809–1865), sixteenth president
of the United States

Mary Todd Lincoln (1818–1882), his wife

Robert Todd Lincoln (1843–1926), son

Edward Baker Lincoln (1846–1850), son

William Wallace Lincoln (1850–1862), son

Thomas "Tad" Lincoln (1853–1871), son

LINCOLN'S FRIENDS
John Todd Stuart, law partner

Joshua Speed, Springfield friend

William de Fleurville, or Florville, his barber

Elizabeth Keckly, Mary's seamstress and confidante

LINCOLN'S OPPONENTS

Senator Stephen A. Douglas, Democrat of Illinois,
presidential opponent, 1860

John C. Breckinridge, presidential opponent, 1860

John Bell, presidential opponent, 1860

George B. McClellan, presidential opponent, 1864

Chief Justice of the United States Roger B. Taney

Fernando Wood, Democratic mayor of New York City

Jefferson Davis, president of the Confederate States of America

Alexander Hamilton Stephens, vice president of the
Confederate States of America

LINCOLN'S CABINET AND OTHER GOVERNMENT OFFICIALS

Hannibal Hamlin of Maine, vice president, 1861–1865

Andrew Johnson of Tennessee, vice president,
March 1865–April 1865

William H. Seward of New York, secretary of state

Salmon P. Chase of Ohio, secretary of the treasury

Simon Cameron of Pennsylvania, secretary of war, 1861–1862

Edwin M. Stanton of Ohio, secretary of war, 1862–1868

Gideon Welles of Connecticut, secretary of the navy

Montgomery Blair of Maryland, postmaster general

Edward Bates of Missouri, attorney general

Charles W. Dana, assistant secretary of war

John G. Nicolay, private secretary to the president

William O. Stoddard, White House clerk

Frederick Seward, private secretary to his father,
the secretary of state

IMPORTANT JOURNALISTS

Frederick Douglass, editor of *Douglass' Monthly*

Horace Greeley, editor of the *New York Tribune*

MILITARY LEADERS (UNION)

General Winfield Scott

General Benjamin F. Butler

General George B. McClellan

General Ambrose E. Burnside

General Joseph Hooker

General George G. Meade

General Henry W. Halleck

General Ulysses S. Grant

General William T. Sherman

Admiral David Dixon Porter

General Nathaniel Banks

General John C. Frémont

General David Hunter

Colonel Robert Gould Shaw

MILITARY LEADERS (CONFEDERATE)
General Robert E. Lee

MEMBERS OF CONGRESS DEBATING THE THIRTEENTH AMENDMENT
Senator Charles Sumner (Massachusetts)

Senator Reverdy Johnson (Maryland)

Senator Lyman Trumbull (Illinois)

Senator Ira Harris (New York)

Speaker of the House Thaddeus Stevens (Pennsylvania)

Representative August King (Maryland)

Representative James S. Rollins (Maryland)

Representative Lazarus Powell (New York)

Representative Anson Herrick (New York)

Representative John Todd Stuart (Illinois)

Representative Samuel "Sunset" Cox (Ohio)

Representative Thomas S. Shannon (Connecticut)

Representative Willard Saulsbury (Connecticut)

Representative George Julian (Indiana)

Representative Alexander Coffroth (Pennsylvania)

LINCOLN ASSASSINATION CONSPIRATORS AND WITNESSES

John Wilkes Booth

Lewis Paine, alias Lewis Powell

George Atzerodt

Major Henry Rathbone

Clara Harris

✶ CHRONOLOGY IN BRIEF ✶

1809   Abraham Lincoln born February 12 in Kentucky.

1820   Missouri Compromise prohibited slavery above the latitude of 36°30′.

1816   Lincoln family moves to Indiana.

1828   Lincoln makes first flatboat trip down Mississippi River to New Orleans, probably sees first slave auction.

1831   Lincoln family moves from Indiana to Coles County, Illinois. Lincoln makes second flatboat journey down the Mississippi to New Orleans. Leaves his family's home and moves himself to village of New Salem for next six years.

1832   Lincoln defeated in his first try for elective office as a Whig candidate for the Illinois House of Representatives.

1833   Slavery abolished in British Empire.

1834   Lincoln wins seat in Illinois State Legislature with "the highest vote cast for any candidate"; begins study of law.

1836   Lincoln obtains license to practice law. Reelected to Illinois State Legislature, he finishes first among seventeen candidates.

1837   Lincoln moves to Springfield, the new site of the Illinois state capital; in legislature, he is one of two signers of a brief protest against both slavery and abolitionism. (Lincoln is twenty-eight years old, the midpoint of his life.)

1838   Lincoln reelected to Illinois State Legislature, finishing with highest vote of seven winners.

1839   Lincoln admitted to practice before the U.S. Circuit Court; meets Mary Ann Todd.

1840   Despite opposition from her family, Lincoln becomes engaged to Mary Todd. Reelected to the state legislature, but with lowest vote in the county, he vows not to seek reelection in 1842.

1841   Breaks engagement to Mary Todd. Returning from trip to Louisville, he observes chained slaves being sold downriver.

1842   Reunites with Mary Todd. They marry on November 4.

1843   Lincoln loses Whig nomination for U.S. Congress; chosen Whig elector for the 1844 presidential race. His son Robert Todd Lincoln (the only Lincoln child to survive to adulthood, past teenage years—two of them didn't even make it to teens) born August 1.

1844   Lincoln starts own law practice; campaigns vigorously for his hero, Henry Clay, for president.

1845   His law practice grows. He's promised next Whig nomination to Congress.

1846   As Whig nominee for Congress, Lincoln wins election; son Edward Baker Lincoln born March 10.

1847   He takes his seat in Congress December 6. Under political arrangement among Whigs, he is a one-term-only congressman and will not be offered renomination.

1849   He votes in the House to ban slavery from the western territories and the District of Columbia. His congressional term expires.

1850   His son Eddie dies February 1. Lincoln resumes legal career. His third son, William Wallace Lincoln, is born December 21.

1852   Chosen a Whig elector in the presidential race.

1853   His fourth and last son, Thomas "Tad" Lincoln, born April 4.

1854   Reenters political arena to stay. Speaks against passage of the Kansas-Nebraska Act, opposing Act's champion, Senator Stephen A. Douglas. Reelected to Illinois State Legislature, he declines the seat to make himself eligible for next U.S. senator selection.

1855   In a vote by the state legislature, Lincoln loses election for U.S. senator by a handful of votes.

1856   Lincoln helps launch Republican Party in Illinois; at first Republican Party National Convention, though eleven states support him for vice presidential nomination, he loses to William I. Dayton.

1857   Law practice grows; he speaks out against Dred Scott Decision when Supreme Court rules negroes ineligible for U.S. citizenship. He begins to be described as likely "successor" to Democratic senator Stephen A. Douglas.

1858   Lincoln wins Republican nomination for Illinois's U.S. Senate seat in June; campaigns vigorously, including engaging in series of seven debates against opponent Douglas, which draw record crowds. Republicans win popular vote, but winner will be selected by vote in Illinois State Legislature, which is Democratically controlled.

1859   Douglas officially wins legislature's vote for U.S. senator, 54 to 46. Lincoln seeks publisher for transcripts of the debates, continues his legal business.

1859   John Brown leads armed raid on federal arsenal at Harpers Ferry, Virginia, to incite slave insurrection, but is captured, tried, and executed.

1860   Lincoln speaks in February before fifteen hundred people
        at the Great Hall of Cooper Union in Manhattan. Lincoln-
        Douglas debates are published. Illinois legislature pledges
        its delegates to Lincoln for president May 10; national
        convention nominates him on May 18. Though his name does
        not appear on the ballot in ten states, he wins presidential
        election with 180 electoral votes on November 6.

1861   Moves to Washington, D.C.; chooses cabinet officials,
        including former convention rivals; sworn in to office on
        March 4. Civil War starts with attack on Fort Sumter, April 12.

1862   Names Edwin M. Stanton as new Secretary of War on
        January 13. Lincoln's eleven-year-old son Willie dies in
        White House February 20 after a brief illness. Lincoln
        writes draft of the Emancipation Proclamation in July but
        withholds it pending Union victory. Five days after Battle
        of Antietam, September 17, he issues proclamation, which
        abolishes slavery in states still in rebellion January 1. In
        annual message to Congress December 1, he proposes
        constitutional amendment for gradual, compensated
        emancipation in loyal slave states, suggests colonization of
        freed African Americans.

1863   Lincoln signs final Emancipation Proclamation January 1.
        Union loses Battle of Chancellorsville in May but triumphs
        at Gettysburg and Vicksburg in July. Lincoln delivers most
        famous presidential address at Gettysburg on November 19.

1864   Lincoln meets General Ulysses Grant for the first time
        at a White House reception March 8; four days later,
        he promotes him to general in chief. On April 4, U.S.
        Senate passes resolution for Thirteenth Amendment to
        Constitution, which would abolish slavery throughout
        the United States; House of Representatives takes up
        amendment on May 31. Lincoln nominated June 8 for
        second term by the new National Union Party, a coalition

of Republicans and War Democrats, with Andrew Johnson for vice president. Lincoln wins reelection in November.

1865   On January 31 the House finally passes, by three votes, the Thirteenth Amendment and sends it to the states, where it is ratified eight months later. On February 3 Lincoln meets Confederate peace commissioners at Hampton Roads Conference. He gives second inaugural address March 4. Confederate General Robert E. Lee surrenders to Grant April 1, effectively ending Civil War. Lincoln is fatally shot at a Washington theater on April 14, dying on the morning of April 15.

This chronology is drawn in part from the more detailed version in the book Lincoln on Democracy, *edited by Mario M. Cuomo and Harold Holzer, a Cornelia & Michael Bessie Book, an imprint of HarperCollins Publishers, published 2004. Reprinted by permission.*

PRELIMINARY EMANCIPATION PROCLAMATION

Issued September 22, 1862

BY THE PRESIDENT OF
THE UNITED STATES OF AMERICA:

A Proclamation.

I, Abraham Lincoln, President of the United States of America, and Commander-in-Chief of the Army and Navy thereof, do hereby proclaim and declare that hereafter, as heretofore, the war will be prosecuted for the object of practically restoring the constitutional relation between the United States, and each of the States, and the people thereof, in which States that relation is, or may be, suspended or disturbed.

That it is my purpose, upon the next meeting of Congress to again recommend the adoption of a practical measure tendering pecuniary aid to the free acceptance or rejection of all slave States, so called, the people whereof may not then be in rebellion against the United States and which States may then have voluntarily adopted, or thereafter may voluntarily adopt, immediate or gradual abolishment of slavery within their respective limits; and that the effort to colonize persons of African descent, with their consent, upon this continent, or elsewhere, with the previously obtained consent of the Governments existing there, will be continued.

That on the first day of January in the year of our Lord, one thousand eight hundred and sixty-three, all persons held as slaves within any State, or designated part of a State, the people whereof shall then be in rebellion against the United States shall be then, thenceforward, and forever free; and the executive government of the United States, including the military and naval authority thereof, will recognize and maintain the freedom of such persons, and will do no act or acts to repress such persons, or any of them, in any efforts they may make for their actual freedom.

That the executive will, on the first day of January aforesaid, by proclamation, designate the States, and part of States, if any, in which the people thereof respectively, shall then be in rebellion against the United States; and the fact that any State, or the people thereof shall, on that day be, in good faith represented in the Congress of the United States, by members chosen thereto, at elections wherein a majority of the qualified voters of such State shall have participated, shall, in the absence of strong countervailing testimony, be deemed conclusive evidence that such State and the people thereof, are not then in rebellion against the United States.

That attention is hereby called to an Act of Congress entitled "An Act to make an additional Article of War" approved March

13, 1862, and which act is in the words and figure following:

"Be it enacted by the Senate and House of Representatives of the United States of America in Congress assembled, That hereafter the following shall be promulgated as an additional article of war for the government of the army of the United States, and shall be obeyed and observed as such:

"Article—All officers or persons in the military or naval service of the United States are prohibited from employing any of the forces under their respective commands for the purpose of returning fugitives from service or labor, who may have escaped from any persons to whom such service or labor is claimed to be due, and any officer who shall be found guilty by a court martial of violating this article shall be dismissed from the service.

"Sec. 2. And be it further enacted, That this act shall take effect from and after its passage."

Also to the ninth and tenth sections of an act entitled "An Act to suppress Insurrection, to punish Treason and Rebellion, to seize and confiscate property of rebels, and for other purposes," approved July 17, 1862, and which sections are in the words and figures following:

"Sec. 9. And be it further enacted, That all slaves of persons who shall hereafter be engaged in rebellion against the government of the United States, or who shall in any way give aid or comfort thereto, escaping from such persons and taking refuge within the lines of the army; and all slaves captured from such persons or deserted by them and coming under the control of the government of the United States; and all slaves of such persons found on (or) being within any place occupied by rebel forces and afterwards occupied by the forces of the United States, shall

be deemed captives of war, and shall be forever free of their servitude and not again held as slaves.

"Sec. 10. And be it further enacted, That no slave escaping
into any State, Territory, or the District of Columbia, from any
other State, shall be delivered up, or in any way impeded or hin-
dered of his liberty, except for crime, or some offence against the
laws, unless the person claiming said fugitive shall first make
oath that the person to whom the labor or service of such fugitive is alleged to be due is his lawful owner, and has not borne
arms against the United States in the present rebellion, nor in
any way given aid and comfort thereto; and no person engaged
in the military or naval service of the United States shall, under
any pretence whatever, assume to decide on the validity of the
claim of any person to the service or labor of any other person, or
surrender up any such person to the claimant, on pain of being
dismissed from the service."

And I do hereby enjoin upon and order all persons engaged
in the military and naval service of the United States to observe,
obey, and enforce, within their respective spheres of service, the
act, and sections above recited.

And the executive will in due time recommend that all citizens of the United States who shall have remained loyal thereto
throughout the rebellion, shall (upon the restoration of the constitutional relation between the United States, and their respective States, and people, if that relation shall have been suspended
or disturbed) be compensated for all losses by acts of the United
States, including the loss of slaves.

In witness whereof, I have hereunto set my hand, and caused
the seal of the United States to be affixed.

Done at the City of Washington this twenty-second day of September, in the year of our Lord, one thousand, eight hundred and sixty-two, and of the Independence of the United States the eighty seventh.

Abraham Lincoln
By the President
William H. Seward
Secretary of State

✳ FINAL EMANCIPATION PROCLAMATION ✳

Issued January 1, 1863

BY THE PRESIDENT OF
THE UNITED STATES OF AMERICA:

A Proclamation.

Whereas, on the twenty-second day of September, in the year of our Lord one thousand eight hundred and sixty-two, a proclamation was issued by the President of the United States, containing, among other things, the following, to wit:

"That on the first day of January, in the year of our Lord one thousand eight hundred and sixty-three, all persons held as slaves within any State or designated part of a State, the people whereof shall then be in rebellion against the United States, shall be then, thenceforward, and forever free; and the Executive Government of the United States, including the military and naval authority thereof, will recognize and maintain the freedom of such persons, and will do no act or acts to repress such persons, or any of them, in any efforts they may make for their actual freedom.

"That the Executive will, on the first day of January aforesaid, by proclamation, designate the States and parts of States, if any, in which the people thereof, respectively, shall then be in rebellion against the United States; and the fact that any State, or the people thereof, shall on that day be, in good faith, represented in the Congress of the United States by members chosen thereto at elections wherein a majority of the qualified voters of such State shall have participated, shall, in the absence of strong countervailing testimony, be deemed conclusive evidence that such State, and the people thereof, are not then in rebellion against the United States."

Now, therefore I, Abraham Lincoln, President of the United States, by virtue of the power in me vested as Commander-in-Chief, of the Army and Navy of the United States in time of actual armed rebellion against the authority and government of the United States, and as a fit and necessary war measure for suppressing said rebellion, do, on this first day of January, in the year of our Lord one thousand eight hundred and sixty-three, and in accordance with my purpose so to do publicly proclaimed for the full period of one hundred days, from the day first above mentioned, order and designate as the States and parts of States wherein the people thereof respectively, are this day in rebellion against the United States, the following, to wit:

Arkansas, Texas, Louisiana, (except the Parishes of St. Bernard, Plaquemines, Jefferson, St. John, St. Charles, St. James Ascension, Assumption, Terrebonne, Lafourche, St. Mary, St. Martin, and Orleans, including the City of New Orleans) Mississippi, Alabama, Florida, Georgia, South Carolina, North Carolina, and Virginia, (except the forty-eight counties designated as West Virginia, and also the counties of Berkley,

Accomac, Northampton, Elizabeth City, York, Princess Ann, and Norfolk, including the cities of Norfolk and Portsmouth), and which excepted parts, are for the present, left precisely as if this proclamation were not issued.

And by virtue of the power, and for the purpose aforesaid, I do order and declare that all persons held as slaves within said designated States, and parts of States, are, and henceforward shall be free; and that the Executive government of the United States, including the military and naval authorities thereof, will recognize and maintain the freedom of said persons.

And I hereby enjoin upon the people so declared to be free to abstain from all violence, unless in necessary self-defence; and I recommend to them that, in all cases when allowed, they labor faithfully for reasonable wages.

And I further declare and make known, that such persons of suitable condition, will be received into the armed service of the United States to garrison forts, positions, stations, and other places, and to man vessels of all sorts in said service.

And upon this act, sincerely believed to be an act of justice, warranted by the Constitution, upon military necessity, I invoke the considerate judgment of mankind, and the gracious favor of Almighty God.

In witness whereof, I have hereunto set my hand and caused the seal of the United States to be affixed.

Done at the City of Washington, this first day of January, in the year of our Lord one thousand eight hundred and sixty three, and of the Independence of the United States of America the eighty-seventh.

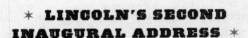

★ LINCOLN'S SECOND INAUGURAL ADDRESS ★

Delivered March 4, 1865

FELLOW COUNTRYMEN:

At this second appearing to take the oath of the presidential office, there is less occasion for an extended address than there was at the first. Then, a statement, somewhat in detail, of a course to be pursued, seemed fitting and proper. Now, at the expiration of four years, during which public declarations have been constantly called forth, on every point and phase of the great contest which still absorbs the attention, and engrosses the energies of the nation, little that is new could be presented. The progress of our arms, upon which all else chiefly depends, is as well known to the public as to myself; and it is, I trust, reasonably satisfactory and encouraging to all. With high hope for the future, no prediction in regard to it is ventured.

On the occasion corresponding to this four years ago, all thoughts were anxiously directed to an impending civil war. All dreaded it—all sought to avert it. While the inaugural address was being delivered from this place, devoted altogether to *saving* the Union without war, insurgent agents were in the city seeking to *destroy* it without war—seeking to dissolve the Union, and divide effects, by negotiation. Both parties deprecated war; but one of them would *make* war rather than let the nation survive; and the other would *accept* war rather than let it perish. And the war came.

One-eighth of the whole population were colored slaves, not distributed generally over the Union, but localized in the southern half part of it. These slaves constituted a peculiar, and powerful interest. All knew that this interest was, somehow, the cause of the war. To strengthen, perpetuate and extend this interest, was the object for which the insurgents would rend the Union, even by war; while the government claimed no right to do more, than to restrict the territorial enlargement of it. Neither party expected for the war, the magnitude, or the duration, which it has already attained. Neither anticipated that the cause of the conflict might cease with, or even before, the conflict itself should cease. Each looked for an easier triumph, and a result less fundamental and astounding. Both read the same Bible, and pray to the same God; and each invokes His aid against the other. It may seem strange that any men should dare to ask a just God's assistance in wringing their bread from the sweat of other men's faces; but let us judge not, that we be not judged. The prayers of both could not be answered—that of neither, has been answered fully. The Almighty has His own purposes. "Woe unto the world because of offences! for it must needs be that offences come; but woe to that man by whom the offence cometh." If we shall suppose that American slavery is one of those offences which, in the providence of God, must needs come, but which, having continued through His appointed time,

He now wills to remove; and that He gives to both north and south this terrible war, as the woe due to those by whom the offence came, shall we discern therein any departure from those divine attributes which the believers in a living God always ascribe to Him? Fondly do we hope—fervently do we pray—that this mighty scourge of war may speedily pass away. Yet, if God wills that it continue until all the wealth piled by the bondman's two hundred and fifty years of unrequited toil shall be sunk, and until every drop of blood drawn with the lash, shall be paid by another drawn with the sword, as was said three thousand years ago, so still it must be said, "the judgments of the Lord are true and righteous altogether."

With malice toward none; with charity for all; with firmness in the right, as God gives us to see the right, let us strive on to finish the work we are in; to bind up the nation's wounds; to care for him who shall have borne the battle, and for his widow, and his orphan—to do all which may achieve and cherish, a just and a lasting peace, among ourselves, and with all nations.

✷ NOTES ✷

ONE

"My education had been sadly neglected": Kenneth J. Winkle, *The Young Eagle: The Rise of Abraham Lincoln* (Dallas, TX: Taylor Trade Publishing, 2001), 123.

Lincoln seldom glimpsed: Douglas L. Wilson and Rodney O. Davis, eds., *Herndon's Informants: Letters, Interviews, and Statements About Abraham Lincoln* (Urbana: University of Illinois Press, 1990), 240.

"held out a great promise": Roy P. Basler, ed., *The Collected Works of Abraham Lincoln*, vol. 4 (New Brunswick, NJ: Rutgers University Press, 1953–55), 235–36.

"which gave me more pleasure": Basler, ed., *The Collected Works of Abraham Lincoln*, vol. 3, 512.

THREE

"precisely like droves of horses": Basler, *The Collected Works of Abraham Lincoln*, vol. 2, 253.

FOUR

"let us beware, lest we": Mario M. Cuomo and Harold Holzer, eds., *Lincoln on Democracy* (New York: HarperCollins, 1990), 40.

"a house divided against itself": Basler, *The Collected Works of Abraham Lincoln*, vol. 2, 461.

"there is a physical difference": Basler, *The Collected Works of Abraham Lincoln*, vol. 3, 145–46.

"MUZZLING THE CANNON": Basler, *The Collected Works of Abraham Lincoln*, vol. 2, 77.

"THIS EXPRESSED MY IDEA": Cuomo and Holzer, *Lincoln on Democracy*, 121.

"THAT IS THE REAL ISSUE": Basler, *The Collected Works of Abraham Lincoln*, vol. 3, 315–16.

FIVE

"AGREED WITH US IN THINKING": Ibid., 502.

"SURELY HEADING FOR A 'DISAPPOINTMENT'": Harold Holzer, *Lincoln at Cooper Union: The Speech that Made Abraham Lincoln President* (New York: Simon & Schuster, 2004), 59.

"THERE WAS ABSOLUTELY NO MORE PITY": Ibid., 187.

SIX

"CREPT INTO WASHINGTON LIKE A THIEF": Harold Holzer, *Lincoln President-Elect* (New York: Simon & Schuster, 2008), 398.

"WITH A RING TO HIS VOICE": Ibid., 414.

"THE TUG HAS TO COME": Basler, *The Collected Works of Abraham Lincoln*, vol. 4, 150.

"HOLD FAST, AS WITH A CHAIN": Ibid., 151.

"THOUSANDS OF LINCOLNITES": Holzer, *Lincoln President-Elect*, 449.

"ESCORTING A PRISONER TO HIS DOOM": Ibid., 448.

"YOU NOT ONLY HEARD EVERY WORD": Ibid., 455.

"WE ARE NOT ENEMIES": Basler, *The Collected Works of Abraham Lincoln*, vol. 4, 271.

"CIVIL WAR WILL BE INAUGURATED": Cuomo and Holzer, *Lincoln on Democracy*, 201.

SEVEN

"YOU EXPRESS GREAT HORROR": Basler, *The Collected Works of Abraham Lincoln*, vol. 4, 341–42.

"STINK IN THE NOSTRILS": Benjamin Brown French, *Witness to the Young Republic: A Yankee's Journal 1828–1870*, eds. Donald B. Cole and John J. McDonough (Hanover, NH: University Press of New England, 1989), 382.

"IT WOULD NEVER DO": Don E. Fehrenbacher and Virginia Fehrenbacher, *Recollected Words of Abraham Lincoln* (Stanford, CA: Stanford University Press, 1996), 194.

"RAPIDLY DISINTEGRATE": Harold Holzer, *Emancipating Lincoln: The Emancipation Proclamation in Text, Context, and Memory* (Cambridge, MA: Harvard University Press, 2012), 28.

EIGHT

"OH, WHAT A TERRIBLE SLAUGHTER": Fehrenbacher and Fehrenbacher, *Recollected Words of Abraham Lincoln*, 429.

"THOSE DREADFUL DAYS!": Ibid., 429.

"MY PARAMOUNT OBJECT IN THIS STRUGGLE": Basler, *The Collected Works of Abraham Lincoln*, vol. 5, 388–89.

"WHEN THE REBEL ARMY": David Donald, ed., *Inside Lincoln's Cabinet: The Civil War Diaries of Salmon P. Chase* (New York: Longmans, Green & Co., 1954), 150.

CITING HIS POWERS AS "COMMANDER-IN-CHIEF": Basler, *The Collected Works of Abraham Lincoln*, vol. 5, 433–434.

"COME FORTH MORE SLOWLY": Ibid., 444.

"I HOPE FOR GREATER GAIN": Harold Holzer, *Lincoln Seen and Heard* (Lawrence, KS: University Press of Kansas, 2000), 187.

"WHAT I DID, I DID AFTER": Basler, *The Collected Works of Abraham Lincoln*, vol. 5, 438.

"ONE MIDSUMMER DAY SEEMS TO REPAIR": Herbert Mitgang, ed., *Lincoln as They Saw Him* (New York: Rinehart & Co., 1955), 325.

"GOD BLESS YOU FOR A *GOOD DEED*!": Harold Holzer, *Dear Mr. Lincoln: Letters to the President* (New York: Addison-Wesley, 1993), 234.

"WE ARE ON THE BRINK": Stefan Lorant, *Lincoln: A Picture Story of His Life*, rev. ed. (New York: W. W. Norton, 1969), 181.

NINE

"HE WILL STAND BY THE PROCLAMATION": Michael Vorenberg, "The Thirteenth Amendment Enacted," in *Lincoln and Freedom: Slavery, Emancipation, and the Thirteenth Amendment*, eds. Harold Holzer and Sarah Vaughn Gabbard (Carbondale, IL: Southern Illinois University Press, 2007), 107.

"THE SOUTH HAD FAIR WARNING": Francis B. Carpenter, *Six Months at the White House with Abraham Lincoln: The Story of a Picture* (New York: Hurd & Houghton, 1866), 87.

"FELLOW-CITIZENS, WE CANNOT ESCAPE": Basler, *The Collected Works of Abraham Lincoln*, vol. 5, 537.

"I HAVE BEEN SHAKING HANDS": Francis B. Carpenter, *Six Months at the White House*, 110, 286.

"LAW AND THE SWORD": Philip S. Foner and Yuval Taylor, eds., *Frederick Douglass: Selected Speeches and Letters*, orig. pub. 1950–75 (Chicago: Lawrence Hull Books, 1999), 523–525.

"No human power can subdue": Vorenberg, "The Thirteenth Amendment Enacted," 76.

"the central act of my administration": Fehrenbacher and Fehrenbacher, *Recollected Words of Abraham Lincoln*, 90.

TEN

"lie in the woods": Holzer, *Lincoln Seen and Heard*, 86.

"to arm, uniform, equip": James I. Robertson Jr., *Soldiers Blue and Gray* (Columbia, SC: University of South Carolina Press, 1988), 31.

Lincoln's War Department: Vorenberg, "The Thirteenth Amendment Enacted," 120.

"I am told you": Basler, *The Collected Works of Abraham Lincoln*, vol. 6, 149–50.

"all the slaves you can": Vorenberg, "The Thirteenth Amendment Enacted," 123.

"essential service in finishing": Basler, *The Collected Works of Abraham Lincoln*, vol. 6, 239.

"[I]f there can be negroes enough": Vorenberg, "The Thirteenth Amendment Enacted," 126.

"I am a soldier now": Ibid., 122.

"give the same protection": Basler, *The Collected Works of Abraham Lincoln*, vol. 6, 357.

"First—You must give": Holzer, *Lincoln Seen and Heard*, 203–204.

"I assure you, Mr. Douglass": Holzer, *Lincoln Seen and Heard*, 203–204.

"Your golden opportunity is gone": Basler, *The Collected Works of Abraham Lincoln*, vol. 6, 327–28.

"[W]e can be as secluded": Mark E. Neely, Jr. and Harold Holzer, *The Lincoln Family Album: Photographs from the Personal Collection of an American Family*, orig. pub. 1990, rev. ed. (Carbondale, IL: Southern Illinois University Press, 2006), 64.

"although colored": Frank J. Williams and Michael Burkhimer, eds., *The Mary Lincoln Enigma: Historians on America's Most Controversial First Lady* (Carbondale, IL: Southern Illinois University Press, 2012), 53.

Mary admitted she sometimes felt: Neely and Holzer, *The Lincoln Family Album*, 61.

ELEVEN

"dislike the Emancipation Proclamation": Basler, *The Collected Works of Abraham Lincoln*, vol. 6, 406–10.

"A MIND BOTH STRONG": Cuomo and Holzer, *Lincoln on Democracy*, 288.

"WORTHY TO BE INSCRIBED": Ibid., xxxiv.

"FOUR SCORE AND SEVEN YEARS": Basler, *The Collected Works of Abraham Lincoln*, vol. 7, 222–23.

"THOSE WHO HAVE TASTED": Basler, *The Collected Works of Abraham Lincoln*, vol. 6, 358.

"HIS AFRICAN AMERICAN AIDE": John E. Washington, *They Knew Lincoln* (New York: E. P. Dutton, 1942).

"THE NATION WILL REJOICE": Holzer, *Dear Mr. Lincoln*, 320–21.

TWELVE

"IF THE REBELLION COULD FORCE": Basler, *The Collected Works of Abraham Lincoln*, vol. 8, 101.

"SLAVE KINGS": Michael Vorenberg, *Final Freedom: The Civil War, the Abolition of Slavery, and the Thirteenth Amendment* (New York: Cambridge University Press, 2001), 91.

ONLY A CONSTITUTIONAL AMENDMENT COULD HELP: Harold Holzer, ed., *The Lincoln Mailbag: America Writes to the President 1860–1861* (Carbondale, IL: Southern Illinois University Press, 1998), 170.

"EVIDENCE CONCLUSIVE ON MR. LINCOLN'S PART": Holzer, *Dear Mr. Lincoln*, 269–70.

"AS A MATTER OF MORALS": Basler, *The Collected Works of Abraham Lincoln*, vol. 7, 500.

WITH THE PEOPLE SO STRONGLY: Basler, *The Collected Works of Abraham Lincoln*, vol. 8, 96.

AND ROBERT T. LINCOLN, AS HE PREFERRED: Ibid., 129.

THIRTEEN

"TO FREE [THE SLAVES]": Vorenberg, *Final Freedom*, 77.

"THE ROOT OF THE ACCURSED TREE": Ibid., 127.

"I CLAIM NOT TO": Ibid., 282.

"[A]S I HAVE OFTEN BEFORE SAID": Basler, *The Collected Works of Abraham Lincoln*, vol. 7, 542–43.

"THE VOICE OF THE PEOPLE": Basler, *The Collected Works of Abraham Lincoln*, vol. 8, 149.

"UNANIMITY OF ACTION": Ibid., 149.

"I LEAVE IT TO YOU": Allen Thorndike Rice, ed, *Reminiscences of Abraham Lincoln by Distinguished Men of His Time* (New York: North American Review, 1886), 585.

"[Y]OUR BROTHER DIED": J. G. Arnold, *The History of Abraham Lincoln and the Overthrow of Slavery* (Chicago: Clarke & Co., 1866), 193.

"WAS PASSED BY CORRUPTION": Vorenberg, "The Thirteenth Amendment Enacted," 182–83.

"ONE OF THE GRANDEST EVENTS": Keller, "'That Which Congress So Nobly Began': The Men Who Passed the Thirteenth Amendment Resolution," in *Lincoln and Freedom: Slavery, Emancipation, and the Thirteenth Amendment*, 201.

FOURTEEN

"SAY TO THE GENTLEMEN": Basler, *The Collected Works of Abraham Lincoln*, vol. 8, 256.

"SHORT OF AN END": Ibid., 279.

"MEN ARE NOT FLATTERED": Ibid., 356.

"I KNOW THAT I AM FREE": William C. Harris, *Lincoln's Last Months* (Cambridge, MA: Harvard University Press, 2004), 205.

"I PASSED LAST NIGHT": Basler, *The Collected Works of Abraham Lincoln*, vol. 8, 387.

"A RIGHTEOUS AND SPEEDY PEACE": Ibid., 399.

"FINDING THEMSELVES SAFELY AT HOME": Ibid., 403.

"NOW, BY GOD, I WILL": Harold Holzer, *The President Is Shot! The Assassination of Abraham Lincoln* (Honesdale, PA: Boyds Mills Press, 2004), 79. Edward Steers Jr., *Blood on the Moon: The Assassination of Abraham Lincoln* (Frankfort: University Press of Kentucky, 2002), 91.

"WE MUST *BOTH*, BE MORE CHEERFUL": Justin G. Turner and Linda Levitt, *Mary Todd Lincoln: Her Life and Letters* (New York: Alfred A. Knopf, 1972), 285.

"A UNION OF HEARTS": Basler, *The Collected Works of Abraham Lincoln*, vol. 8, 413.

"I HATE SLAVERY": Fehrenbacher and Fehrenbacher, *Recollected Words of Abraham Lincoln*, 145.

★ BIBLIOGRAPHY ★

Arnold, J. G. *The History of Abraham Lincoln and the Overthrow of Slavery.* Chicago: Clarke & Co., 1866.

Basler, Roy P., ed. *The Collected Works of Abraham Lincoln.* 8 vols. New Brunswick, NJ: Rutgers University Press, 1953–55.

Carpenter, Francis B. *Six Months at the White House with Abraham Lincoln: The Story of a Picture.* New York: Hurd & Houghton, 1866.

Cole, Donald B., and John J. McDonough, eds. *Witness to the Young Republic: A Yankee's Journal [Benjamin Brown French], 1828–1870.* Hanover, NH: University Press of New England, 1989.

Cuomo, Mario M., and Harold Holzer, eds. *Lincoln on Democracy.* New York: Harper-Collins, 1990.

Donald, David, ed. *Inside Lincoln's Cabinet: The Civil War Diaries of Salmon P. Chase.* New York: Longmans, Green & Co., 1954.

Fehrenbacher, Don E., and Virginia Fehrenbacher, *Recollected Words of Abraham Lincoln.* Stanford, CA: Stanford University Press, 1996.

Foner, Eric. *The Fiery Trial: Abraham Lincoln and American Slavery.* New York: W. W. Norton, 2010.

Foner, Philip S., and Yuval Taylor, eds. *Frederick Douglass: Selected Speeches and Letters,* orig. pub. 1950–75. Chicago: Lawrence Hull Books, 1999.

Harris, William C. *Lincoln's Last Months.* Cambridge, MA: Harvard University Press, 2004.

Holzer, Harold. *Dear Mr. Lincoln: Letters to the President.* New York: Addison-Wesley, 1993.

——————————. *Emancipating Lincoln: The Emancipation Proclamation in Text, Context, and Memory.* Cambridge, MA: Harvard University Press, 2012.

——————————. *Lincoln at Cooper Union: The Speech that Made Abraham Lincoln President.* New York: Simon & Schuster, 2004.

——————————. *Lincoln President-Elect*. New York: Simon & Schuster, 2008.

——————————. *Lincoln Seen and Heard*. Lawrence, KS: University Press of Kansas, 2000.

——————————. *The President Is Shot! The Assassination of Abraham Lincoln*. Honesdale, PA: Boyds Mills Press, 2004.

Keller, Ron J. "'That Which Congress So Nobly Began': The Men Who Passed the Thirteenth Amendment Resolution." In *Lincoln and Freedom: Slavery, Freedom, and the Thirteenth Amendment*, eds. Harold Holzer and Sarah Vaughn Gabbard, 195–212. Carbondale: Southern Illinois University Press, 2007.

Lorant, Stefan. *Lincoln: A Picture Story of His Life*, rev. ed. New York: W. W. Norton, 1969.

Mitgang, Herbert, ed. *Lincoln as They Saw Him*. New York: Rinehart & Co., 1955.

Neely, Mark E., Jr., and Harold Holzer. *The Lincoln Family Album: Photographs from the Personal Collection of an American Family*, orig. pub. 1990, rev. ed. Carbondale: Southern Illinois University Press, 2006.

Rice, Allen Thorndike, ed. *Reminiscences of Abraham Lincoln by Distinguished Men of His Time*. New York: North American Review, 1886.

Robertson, James I., Jr. *Soldiers Blue and Gray*. Columbia: University of South Carolina Press, 1988.

Steers, Edward, Jr. *Blood on the Moon: The Assassination of Abraham Lincoln*. Frankfort: University Press of Kentucky, 2002.

Turner, Justin G., and Linda Levitt. *Mary Todd Lincoln: Her Life and Letters*. New York: Alfred A. Knopf, 1972.

Vorenberg, Michael. *Final Freedom: The Civil War, the Abolition of Slavery, and the Thirteenth Amendment*. New York: Cambridge University Press, 2001.

——————————. "The Thirteenth Amendment Enacted." In *Lincoln and Freedom: Slavery, Freedom, and the Thirteenth Amendment*, eds. Harold Holzer and Sarah Vaughn Gabbard, 180–194. Carbondale: Southern Illinois University Press, 2007.

Washington, John E. *They Knew Lincoln*. New York: E. P. Dutton, 1942.

Williams, Frank J., and Michael Burkhimer, eds. *The Mary Lincoln Enigma: Historians on America's Most Controversial First Lady*. Carbondale: Southern Illinois University Press, 2012.

Wilson, Douglas L., and Rodney O. Davis, eds. *Herndon's Informants: Letters, Interviews, and Statements About Abraham Lincoln*. Urbana: University of Illinois Press, 1990.

Winkle, Kenneth J. *The Young Eagle: The Rise of Abraham Lincoln*. Dallas, TX: Taylor Trade Publishing, 2001.

✳ ACKNOWLEDGMENTS ✳

The author wishes to thank the scholars whose work on slavery, emancipation, and the fight to pass the Thirteenth Amendment to the Constitution informed this book, particularly: Michael Vorenberg, Allen Guelzo, Mark Neely, David Blight, Gabor Boritt, David H. Donald, Eric Foner, William C. Harris, Ron Keller, and the late John Hope Franklin. For permission to publish a number of important illustrations, we express our appreciation to Cindy VanHorn and Kara Vetter of the Lincoln National Collection at the Indiana State Museum, and to John Meko of the Union League of Philadelphia.

Gratitude goes too to Esther Margolis and Geri Thoma for making this book possible. To Bethany Larson for helping guide the manuscript into print, and to Kraig Smith and Becky Schear for their usual patience and assistance in the office.

And special thanks to Doris Kearns Goodwin for writing the volume that inspired Steven Spielberg's film, to Mr. Spielberg for making the picture, and above all to my friend Tony Kushner, who wrote the screenplay whose originality and brilliance I can only hope are reflected in this companion book for young readers.

Harold Holzer is one of the country's leading authorities on Abraham Lincoln and the political culture of the Civil War era. A prolific writer and lecturer and frequent guest on television, Holzer serves as chairman of the Lincoln Bicentennial Foundation, successor organization to the U.S. Abraham Lincoln Bicentennial Commission (ALBC), to which he was appointed by President Clinton in 2000, and which he co-chaired from 2001 to 2010. President Bush, in turn, awarded Holzer the National Humanities Medal in 2008. He served as a Content Consultant to the Steven Spielberg film *Lincoln*.

He has authored, co-authored, and edited forty-two books, including *Emancipating Lincoln: The Emancipation Proclamation in Text, Context, and Memory*; *Lincoln at Cooper Union: The Speech That Made Abraham Lincoln President*, which won a coveted second-place Lincoln Prize, the most prestigious award in the field; and three books written especially for young readers: *Father Abraham: Lincoln and His Sons*, named a National Council of Teachers of English Orbis Pictus Honor Book; *The President Is Shot!*, chosen as a notable book by the Children's Book Council and Voice of Youth Advocates; and *Abraham Lincoln, The Writer*, which was included on the Children's Literature Choice List and named a Best Book of the Year by the Bank Street College of Education.